THE
CAMPDEN WONDER

CHIPPING CAMPDEN

The lodge-gate of Campden House is seen in the background on the right

THE
CAMPDEN
WONDER

Edited by
SIR GEORGE CLARK

With chapters by
The Late Viscount Maugham
and
Dr. D. Russell Davis

LONDON
OXFORD UNIVERSITY PRESS
NEW YORK   TORONTO
1959

Oxford University Press, Amen House, London E.C.4

GLASGOW   NEW YORK   TORONTO   MELBOURNE   WELLINGTON
BOMBAY   CALCUTTA   MADRAS   KARACHI   KUALA LUMPUR
CAPE TOWN   IBADAN   NAIROBI   ACCRA

PRINTED IN GREAT BRITAIN

PREFACE

THIS book deals with the seventeenth-century mystery traditionally known as the Campden Wonder. Lord Maugham and Dr. Russell Davis wrote their contributions specially for this volume; I have supplied the remainder of the new text, and the footnotes to the reprinted pieces except those of Paget and Andrew Lang.

Exasperating mischances have delayed the completion of the book for many years, and so it is possible that some name may have been accidentally omitted from the list of acknowledgements on p. xi. If so I offer a sincere apology and the assurance that this is not due to any failure of gratitude.

Three of those who have given help ought to be specially thanked. Mr. H. R. Colman very kindly made some investigations at the Bodleian Library, at Exton, and elsewhere. Mr. A. T. Gaydon's discovery of fresh evidence is described on a later page. He most generously allowed it to be published here instead of appearing under his own name, and he has provided valuable information about Gloucestershire history. Besides helping in many other ways, my wife undertook much of the typing.

G.N.C.

CONTENTS

ILLUSTRATIONS

ACKNOWLEDGEMENTS

THANKS are due to the Deputy Keeper of the Public Records, the Curators of the Bodleian Library, the Visitors of the Ashmolean Museum, and the Governors of Chipping Campden Grammar School for permission to publish materials in their charge, and to the following for answering inquiries or assisting the work in other ways: Mr. Edmund Bardwell, Mr. E. A. B. Barnard, the late Professor J. L. Brierly, Dr. R. W. Chapman, Mr. R. H. Cronin, Mr. C. T. Flower, Mr. Irvine E. Gray, Miss Phyllis Hartnoll, the late Sir William Holdsworth, Sir Harold Spencer Jones, Lady Clare King, Mr. John Masefield, the late Sir Humphrey Milford, Miss Sybil Rosenfeld, Joint Honorary Secretary of the Society for Theatre Research, and the Warden of All Souls College, Oxford.

I

INTRODUCTION

THERE is a novel of Maarten Maartens, more than fifty years old and perhaps forgotten by now, called *The Healers*. At the beginning the hero, a doctor's son, announces that he wishes to become an historian; but his father dissipates this dream with surprisingly little difficulty, and persuades the young man to follow his own profession. His argument is that the study of history mainly consists of 'unravelling lies about crimes'.

Many people still believe this, or something like it; but even if crimes are defined comprehensively enough to include crimes against humanity and crimes against common sense, it is an absurd misrepresentation of what historians do. To say nothing of economic historians, or the historians of thought and of medicine itself, even those political historians who write about murders and conspiracies aim at something very different from satisfying purposeless curiosity. The present volume does not belong to such a dignified species as political history. Its modest aim is to show how in one particular instance historians have unravelled the lies about a crime. It is a detective story, and it abides by the rules of that *genre*: all the evidence is given in full and in the order in which it came to light, so that the reader may form his own conclusions at each stage. The attempted solutions are given fully or in summaries. It would have been easy to provide more entertainment by showing how irresponsibly and carelessly some authors have argued, but the main thread of the book is the positive process by which the truth of the matter has been revealed, so far as it has been revealed at the present time.

By this simple example from one of the lower levels of their activity the book should show what historians do and how they do it. It shows them attending to minute details, as the detectives of fiction do. It shows them assessing the value of human testimony. It shows them resisting the temptation to irrelevance, or succumbing to it. These and such-like elements of the historians' work are familiar, but there is another which constantly needs to be affirmed. Historians are not an isolated body; they are one formation in the vast army of organized thought. It will be observed that this book makes use of expert advice from an astronomer, and students of the theatre. Two of the solutions of the Campden mystery, those of Lord Maugham and Dr. Russell Davis, are published here for the first time: of these writers the one was Lord Chancellor and the other is a medical psychologist. Each of them applies professional knowledge to the case, and each derives professional knowledge from it. Thus historians draw upon the resources of experts whose primary concern is not with the past but the present, and in exchange they prepare materials for these other workers. And just as history has its place in the universal life of thought, each historian is more than an individual artist whose product is self-contained. He borrows

from the accumulated riches of predecessors and con‚
temporaries in his own and many other fields; he makes his
contemporaries and their successors free of his own new
contributions to the common stock. In his capacity as a
social being he need not quail before the knock‚down
argument of the healers. If this can be shown in a detective
story it is many times more evident in the more exalted
branches of historical study.

The ugly story which we have to present has its setting in
Chipping Campden, one of the most beautiful of English
market‚towns, in Gloucestershire under the high escarpment
of the Cotswolds. The wide stone‚built street, with its
market‚house, still looks much as it did in 1660, the year of
the happy Restoration of King Charles II, when the story
begins. A short way from the eastern end of the street rises
the great tower of the church, dominating the town on one
side, and on the other the ruins of the once magnificent
Campden House. The house was already in ruins then. It
was built about 1613 by Baptist Hicks, the first Viscount
Campden, whose wealth and title had descended through
his son‚in‚law the second viscount to the third, his grand‚
son. They were royalists. This third viscount was a Cavalier,
and in the civil war the house was garrisoned for the king;
but when the king's troops had to evacuate it, the governor,
Henry Bard, to prevent it from falling into the enemy's hands,
ordered it to be burnt down. The main building was gone.
There remained some outlying fragments, one of which is
an inhabited house now and seems to have been so then.
These remnants, and the whole Campden estate, belonged
to the dowager Lady Campden, Juliana, or more correctly

Julian, the daughter of the original Baptist Hicks, who held them as part of her jointure.

Here we run already into a difficulty. The principal figure in our story was William Harrison, Lady Campden's steward. Several writers have stated that this rich old lady lived in what was left of Campden House, and some have tried to explain the mystery as an episode in the history of her family in those distracted times. There is no denying that the fortunes of all the more substantial people whom we shall have to mention went up and down with the vicissitudes of national affairs. Lady Campden herself had been a correspondent and a supporter of Archbishop Laud;[1] she was forced to 'compound' for her estate at Campden by paying a large sum to the parliament. The vicar of Campden, William Bartholomew, was a hammer of sectaries and, though he escaped being ejected under the Commonwealth, he was harassed. He spent £200 in his defence against charges that were brought against him.[2] On the day when Charles II was proclaimed in London, 15 May 1660, he preached a sermon which he printed and dedicated to his 'very good Lady and Patronesse, Julian Viscountesse Campden', with the title *The Strong Man ejected by a Stronger than He*. We shall mention three knights, one of them a local man and two judges from London. All three of them were knighted, and the two judges were raised to the bench, between the king's return in May and the August evening with which the story begins. Their minds must have been full of the misdoings of the Puritans; their attention, and

[1] See his letter to her about the living of Staughton Magna, which she presented to St. John's College, Oxford: W. Laud, *Works*, vii (1860), 376.   [2] A. G. Matthews, *Walker Revised* (1948), p. 171.

that of their underlings, must have been concentrated on clearing up the confusions left over from the late distur-bances, or so it might appear.

In due course we shall come back to some of these larger issues, but for the present we must beware of assuming that they were anything more than the distant background of our story, contemporary but not connected with it. Although it is highly probable that Lady Campden heard strange tales of her steward, we have no evidence of it. Nor has anyone cited any evidence that she lived in Campden in 1660; and this is open to question.[1] She was buried there twenty years later, and her monument may be seen in the church, but it was at Brooke in Rutland that she died. People of her station commonly had a choice of residences, and she had no need, so far as we know, to live below her means. Before bringing in the lady and her family, or the national history as it affected them and the little world of Campden, we must first look at the story as we find it.

[1] The statement of the anonymous writer on p. 106 below does not specifically mention the house and, in any case, can hardly be called evidence.

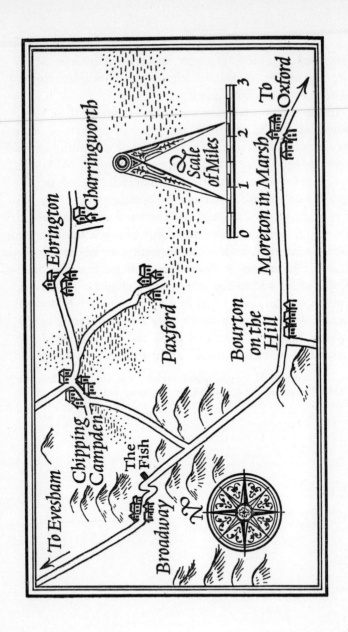

SIR THOMAS OVERBURY'S
TRUE AND PERFECT ACCOUNT
1676

UNTIL the year 1926 the attempts to solve the Campden mystery all started from the facts stated in a single source, a quarto pamphlet of twenty-three pages published in 1676 in the form of a communication from Sir Thomas Overbury to his kinsman Dr. Thomas Shirley. A few other scraps of information were available, as we shall see, but this pamphlet was and still remains the main authority. It immediately established the story as a first-class historical mystery, and apparently it never lost its attraction. There was a second edition in the same year, 1676. There were separate reprints about 1710, in 1743, about 1750, 1767, 1806, and 1904. From 1745 the pamphlet was reprinted in collections along with other matter. Of these the most widely circulated was the long series of historical tracts called *The Harleian Miscellany*. This appeared in 1745; in 1809 there was a second edition, and one or other is to be found in many large libraries at the present day. They brought the story to the notice of educated readers in general. In 1812 the successors of William Cobbett included it in a set of volumes which have been much used ever since by lawyers and people interested in constitutional history, his *State Trials*. These two were the influential reprints: there were others as well as magazine articles extracted from them.[1] The reader will be able to judge from the text which follows whether the pamphlet deserved this literary success. When it first appeared it must have owed something to the names of the writer and the recipient, who were so well known that their identity was not effectively disguised by the conventional device of giving only their initials. It will be useful to preface the text with a few sentences about these two men.

Sir Thomas Overbury lived in the manor house at Bourton on the Hill, six miles from Campden.[2] The estate there had come down to him from his father and his grandfather, and between the two it had belonged to his father's elder brother, also Sir Thomas, who was murdered in the Tower of London in 1613. There is no means of knowing whether the character of the younger Sir Thomas was affected in any way by this fact that his uncle and name-sake, who was something of a poet and something more of a courtier, had been the victim of a horrible crime contrived by the wife of the king's favourite. Whether this had any influence or not, there is no doubt that he was out of the common run of country gentlemen. He was 'a great traveller

[1] These bibliographical particulars are given partly in the late Sir Francis Hyett's useful article 'The Campden Mystery' in *Transactions of the Bristol and Gloucestershire Archaeological Society*, xlix (1927), 195–202, and partly in the British Museum and Bodleian catalogues.

[2] According to Mr. E. A. B. Barnard, who contributed seven articles on Overbury and the mystery to the *Evesham Journal* from Nov. 1925 to Jan. 1926, he was living in 1660 at Weston Subedge, still nearer to Campden, and moved to Bourton later.

beyond the seas' and soon after this time he published a work which shows that he was not averse from stirring up a little dispute about matters of church and state in his part of the world. His pamphlet was called *Queries proposed to the serious Consideration of those who impose upon others in Things of Divine and Supernatural Revelation and persecute any upon the account of Religion*.[1] It appeared in 1677 and George Vernon, the vicar of Bourton on the Hill, replied in a little book called *Ataxiae Obstaculum, an Answer to certain Queries dispersed in some parts of Gloucestershire*. Vernon did not name the author of the queries, but he evidently knew it. He wrote, no doubt rightly, that they were 'chiefly design'd' for 'the unwary countryman'[2] and, from his store of learning, he vindicated the magistrate's coercive power in religion and argued against dissent, 'liberty of conscience', popery, and so forth, The squire replied with a Latin title of his own, *Ratiocinium Vernaculum*,[3] in the following year. We may conclude that Overbury was a man of independent mind and not easily put down.

It has been thought that he was the justice of the peace who examined the witnesses in our case. There does not seem to be any external evidence for this; but Overbury was in the commission of the peace, and his account of the interrogations is so particular that it must originate from some intelligent person who was present. Overbury arranged his matter so clearly that we should have expected him to mention his informant if he had one, and it is a fair

---

[1] I have not seen this work, of which there appears to be no copy in England; but, since the queries are repeated in Vernon's answer, I feel justified in mentioning it here.

[2] p. 85.   [3] This again I have not seen.

inference that this part of his story is first-hand. There is no
need to seek for any explanation of his writing it down and
sending it to Shirley in 1676.[1] He may have had reasons for
not doing it earlier. Some of the characters of the story may
have been alive until near that time, or Overbury may simply
not have had any stimulus to communicating the story
until, as appears from the letter, Shirley asked him in London
to do it when he had gone down to the country. There,
presumably, he had papers to go by. The phrase, 'You may
dispose of it as you please', certainly authorizes Shirley to
show it to other people, and indeed it appears to give him
permission to publish it. Shirley was an author and so it
seems almost sure that Overbury wrote his letter in order
that Shirley might publish it in London.

The pamphlet falls into four parts, a narrative, a statement
by William Harrison, a short covering letter, and some concluding reflections. There is nothing to show that the concluding section was written by Overbury, but it does at any
rate contain further local information. Shirley was not a
local man; he came from Sussex and lived his professional
life in London. He earned a little niche in English constitutional history, for he was the plaintiff in the case of *Shirley* v.
Fagge. For him this was a melancholy experience. He was
physician in ordinary to the king, and he had a flourishing
practice; but he could not forget that he was heir to his
father's estate, and that the estate had been granted during
the civil war to Sir John Fagge. Shirley brought an action
against Fagge before the court of chancery, which decided

---

[1] The identification of the 'T. S. Doctor of Physick' in the title as
Thomas Shirley first appears in A. Wood, *Athenae Oxonienses*, 2nd edn.
(1721), i. 389. The doctor himself used the spelling Sherley.

against him. He appealed to the house of lords; but Fagge
was a member of parliament; the indignant commons
claimed that the appeal to the lords was a breach of their
privileges, and in 1675 Shirley was bundled off and kept in
custody by the serjeant-at-arms for a month or so. It is said
that this disappointment caused him to sink into a morbid
condition, and he only survived until 1678; but it should
be mentioned to his credit that in the short remainder of his
life he did think about other things besides his lawsuit.
He published four translations of continental medical books,
all in two years.[1] As we have seen, he not only received
Overbury's letter, but he probably sent it off to the printer.
Very likely it was his inquiring mind that caused it to be
written. What we know of the recipient as well as the
writer goes to show that this letter ought to be treated, at
least *prima facie*, as a serious authority.

The text which follows has been set up from *The Harleian Miscellany*, iii (1745), 519–26. The footnotes have been
added by the present editor. The Harleian reprint omits the
words from the page facing the title 'Licensed, September
the 8th, 1676. Roger L'Estrange.'

A TRUE and perfect account of the Examination,
Confession, Trial, Condemnation, and Execution of
Joan Perry, and her two sons, *John* and *Richard Perry*, for the
supposed Murder of *William Harrison*, Gent. being one of
the most remarkable Occurrences which hath happened
in the Memory of Man, sent in a Letter (by Sir T. O. of

[1] The titles are given in the *Dictionary of National Biography*. The dedica-
tions, to four noblemen and one knight, give an impression of the trans-
lator's standing.

Burton, in the County of *Gloucester*, Knight, and one of his
Majesty's Justices of the Peace) to T. S. Doctor of Physick in
London. Likewise Mr. *Harrison's* own Account, how he was
conveyed into *Turkey*, and there made a slave for above two
Years; and then, his Master, which bought him there, dying,
how he made his Escape, and what Hardship he endured;
who, at last, through the Providence of God, returned to
England, while he was supposed to be murdered; of which
John Perry his manservant was accused, who falsly impeached
his own Mother and Brother as guilty of the Murder of
his Master; they were all Three arraigned, convicted, and
executed on *Broadway-hills* in Gloucestershire. *London*,
printed for *Rowland Reynolds*, next Arundel-gate, over-
against St. Clement's Church in the Strand, 1676.

Upon *Thursday*, the sixteenth Day of *August*, 1660,
William Harrison, Steward to the Lady Viscountess *Campden*,
at *Campden* in *Gloucestershire*, being about Seventy Years of
Age, walked from *Campden* aforesaid, to *Charringworth*,
about two Miles from thence, to receive his Lady's Rent;
and, not returning so early as formerly, his Wife, Mrs
Harrison, between Eight and Nine of the Clock that
Evening, sent her Servant, *John Perry*, to meet his Master on
the Way from Charringworth; but, neither Mr. *Harrison*, nor
his Servant *John Perry*, returning that Night, the next Morning early, *Edward Harrison*, *William's* Son, went towards
Charringworth to enquire after his Father; when, on the Way,
meeting *Perry* coming thence, and being informed by him
he was not there, they went together to *Ebrington*, a Village
between *Charringworth* and *Campden*, where they were told
by one *Daniel*, that Mr. *Harrison* called at his House the
Evening before, in his Return from *Charringworth*, but

staid not; then they went to Paxford, about Half a Mile thence, where, hearing nothing of Mr. Harrison, they returned towards Campden; and on the Way, hearing of a Hat, Band,[1] and Comb, taken up in the Highway, between Ebrington and Campden, by a poor Woman then leesing[2] in the Field; they sought her out, with whom they found the Hat, Band, and Comb, which they knew to be Mr. Harrison's; and being brought by the Woman to the Place she found the same, in the Highway, between Ebrington and Campden, near unto a great Furz-brake, there they searched for Mr. Harrison, supposing he had been murthered, the Hat and Comb being hacked and cut, and the Band bloody; but nothing more could be there found. The News hereof, coming to Campden, so alarmed the Town, that Men, Women, and Children hasted thence, in Multitudes, to search for Mr. Harrison's supposed dead Body, but all in vain.

Mrs. Harrison's Fears for her Husband, being great, were now much increased; and having sent her Servant Perry, the Evening before, to meet his Master, and he not returning that Night, caused a Suspicion that he had robbed and murthered him; and thereupon the said *Perry* was, the next Day, brought before a Justice of Peace, by whom being examined concerning his Master's Absence, and his own staying out the Night he went to meet him, he gave this Account of himself: That, his Mistress sending him to meet his Master, between Eight and Nine of the Clock in the

[1] We now confine 'bands' in the plural to the pair of strips worn in clerical, legal, or academic dress; but in the seventeenth century 'band' meant a collar of any kind, plain or ornamental.
[2] 'Leesing' is gleaning.

Evening, he went down to *Campden-field*, towards *Charring-worth*, about a Land's Length,[1] where meeting one *William Reed* of *Campden*, he acquainted him with his Errand; and further told him that, it growing dark, he was afraid to go forwards, and would therefore return and fetch his young Master's Horse, and return with him; he did to Mr. *Harrison's* Court-gate,[2] where they parted, and he staid still; one *Pierce* coming by, he went again with him about a Bow's Shot into the Fields, and returned with him likewise to his Master's Gate, where they also parted; and then he, the said *John Perry*, saith, he went into his Master's Hen-roost, where he lay about an Hour, but slept not; and, when the Clock struck Twelve, rose and went towards *Charringworth*, till, a great Mist arising, he lost his Way, and so lay the rest of the Night under a Hedge; and, at Day-break, on Friday Morning went to Charringworth, where he enquired for his Master of one Edward Plaisterer, who told him, he had been with him the Afternoon before, and received three and twenty Pounds of him, but staid not long with him: He then went to *William Curtis* of the same Town, who likewise told him, he heard his Master was at his House the Day before, but, being not at Home, did not see him: After which he saith, he returned homewards, it being about Five of the Clock in the Morning, when, on the Way, he met his Master's Son, with whom he went to *Ebrington* and *Paxford*, & as hath been related.

Read, *Pearce*, *Plaisterer*, and *Curtis*, being examined,

---

[1] Campden field, unenclosed until 1799, was in lands or strips, presumably of the customary length, which was a furlong, more or less.

[2] This need not mean anything grander than the gate to a farmyard or yard of any kind.

affirmed what Perry had said, concerning them, to be true.

Perry being asked by the Justice of Peace, How he, who was afraid to go to Charringworth at Nine of the Clock, became so bold as to go thither at Twelve? Answered, That at Nine of the Clock it was dark, but at Twelve the Moon shone.

Being further asked, Why, returning twice Home, after his Mistress had sent him to meet his Master, and staying till Twelve of the Clock, he went not into the House to know whether his Master were come Home, before he went a third Time, at that Time of Night, to look after him: Answered, That he knew his Master was not come Home, because he saw Light in his Chamber-window, which never used to be there so late when he was at Home.[1]

Yet, notwithstanding this, that *Perry* had said for his Staying forth that Night, it was not thought fit to discharge him till further Inquiry were made after Mr. *Harrison*, and accordingly he continued in Custody at *Campden*, sometimes in an Inn there, and sometimes in the common Prison, from *Saturday*, *August* the Eighteenth, unto the *Friday* following; during which Time, he was again examined at *Campden*, by the aforesaid Justice of Peace, but confessed nothing more than before; nor, at that Time, could any further Discovery be made what was become of Mr. *Harrison*. But it hath been said, that, during his Restraint at *Campden*, he told some, who pressed him to confess what he knew concerning his Master, that a Tinker had killed him; and to others, he said, a Gentleman's Servant of the Neighbour-

---

[1] The chamber must be Harrison's bedroom or office; it seems curious that it should be lighted when he was not in it.

hood had robbed and murdered him; and others, again, he told, That he was murdered, and hid in a Bean-rick in *Campden*, where Search was in vain made for him: At length he gave out, that, were he again carried before the Justice, he would discover that to him he would discover to no Body else: And thereupon he was, Friday, August the twenty-fourth, again brought before the Justice of Peace, who first examined him, and asking whether he would yet confess what was become of his Master; he answered, he was murdered, but not by him: The Justice of Peace then telling him, that, if he knew him to be murdered, he knew likewise by whom he was; so he acknowledged he did; and, being urged to confess what he knew concerning it, affirmed, that it was his Mother and his Brother that had murdered his Master. The Justice of Peace then advised him to consider what he said, telling him, that he feared he might be guilty of his Master's Death, and that he should not draw more innocent Blood on his Head; for what he now charged his Mother and his Brother with might cost them their Lives; but he affirming he spoke nothing but the Truth, and that if he were immediately to die he would justify it; the Justice desired him to declare how and when they did it.

He then told him, that his Mother and his Brother had lain at him, ever since he came into his Master's Service, to help them to Money, telling him, how poor they were, and that it was in his Power to relieve them, by giving them Notice when his Master went to receive his Lady's Rents; for they would then way lay and rob him; and further said, That, upon the *Thursday* Morning his Master went to *Charrington*, going of an Errand into the Town, he met his Brother in the Street, whom he then told whither his Master was going, and, if he way-laid him, he might have his Money: And further said, That, in the Evening his Mistress sent him to meet his Master, he met his Brother in the Street, before his Master's Gate, going, as he said, to meet his Master, and so they went together to the Church-yard about a Stone's Throw from Mr *Harrison*'s Gate, where they parted, he going the Foot-way, Cross the Church-yard, and his Brother keeping the great Road, round the Church; but in the Highway, beyond the Church, met again, and so went together, the Way leading to *Charringworth*, till they came to a Gate about a Bow's Shot from *Campden* Church,[1] that goes into a Ground of the Lady *Campden*'s, called the Conygree[2] (which to those, who have a Key to go through the Garden, is the next Way from that Place to Mr *Harrison*'s House) when they came near unto that Gate, he, the said *John Perry*, saith, he told his Brother, he did believe his Master was just gone into the Conygree (for it was then so dark they could not discern any Man, so as to know him) but perceiving one to go into that Ground, and knowing that there was no Way, but for those who had a Key, through the Gardens, concluded it was his Master; and so told his Brother, if he followed him, he might have his Money, and he, in the mean Time, would walk a Turn in the Fields, which accordingly he did; and then, following his Brother about the Middle of the Conygree, found his Master on the Ground, his Brother upon him, and his Mother standing by; and being asked, Whether his Master was then dead? answered, No, for that, after he came to them, his Master cried, Ah Rogues, will you kill me? At

---

[1] Perhaps a couple of hundred yards.
[2] 'Conygree' means a rabbit-warren.

which he told his Brother, he hoped he would not kill his Master; who replied, *Peasce, Peace, you're a Fool*, and so strangled him; which having done, he took a Bag of Money out of his Pocket, and threw it into his Mother's Lap, and then he and his Brother carried his Master's dead Body into the Garden, adjoining to the Conygree, where they con-sulted what to do with it; and, at length, agreed to throw it into the great Sink, by Wallington's Mill, behind the Garden; but said, his Mother and Brother bade him go up to the Court, next the House, to hearken whether any one were stirring, and they would throw the Body into the Sink:[1] And being asked whether it were there, he said, He knew not, for that he left it in the Garden; but his Mother and Brother said they would throw it there, and, if it were not there, he knew not where it was, for that he returned no more to them, but went into the Court-gate, which goes into the Town, where he met with *John Pearce*, with whom he went into the Field, and again returned with him to his Master's Gate; after which, he went into the Hen-roost, where he lay till Twelve of the Clock that Night, but slept not; and having, when he came from his Mother and Brother, brought with him his Master's Hat, Band, and Comb, which he laid in the Hen-roost, he carried the said Hat, Band, and Comb, and threw them, after he had given them three or four Cuts with his Knife, in the High-way, where they were after found: And being asked, What he intended by so doing? said, He did it, that it might be believed his Master had been there robbed and murdered; and, having thus disposed of his Hat, Band and Comb, he went towards Charringworth, &. as hath been related.

[1] This appears to mean the cesspool for the great house.

Upon this Confession and Accusation, the Justice of Peace gave Order for the apprehending of *Joan* and *Richard Perry*, the Mother and Brother of John Perry, and for search-ing the Sink where Mr. Harrison's Body was said to be thrown, which was accordingly done, but nothing of him could be there found; the Fish-pools likewise, in Campden, were drawn and searched, but nothing could be there found neither; so that some were of Opinion, the Body might be hid in the Ruins of Campden-house, burnt in the late Wars, and not unfit for such a Concealment, where was likewise Search made, but all in vain.

Saturday, August the Twenty-fifth, *Joan* and *Richard Perry*, together with John Perry, were brought before the Justice of Peace, who acquainting the said Joan and Richard with what John had laid to their Charge, they denied all, with many Imprecations on themselves, if they were in the least guilty of any Thing, of which they were accused: But John, on the other Side, affirmed, to their Faces, that he had spoken nothing but the Truth, and that they had murdered his Master; further telling them, that he could never be at Quiet for them, since he came into his Master's Service, being continually followed by them, to help them to Money, which they told him he might do by giving them Notice when his Master went to receive his Lady's Rents; and that he, meeting his Brother *Richard* in *Campden* Town, the *Thursday* Morning his Master went to Charringworth, told him whither he was going, and upon what Errand: *Richard* confessed he met his Brother that Morning, and spoke with him, but nothing passed between them to that Purpose; and both he and his Mother told John he was a Villain to accuse them wrongfully, as he had done; but *John*, on the other Side, affirmed, that he had spoken nothing but the Truth, and would justify it to his Death.

One remarkable Circumstance happened in these Prison-ers Return from the Justice of Peace's House to Campden, viz. *Richard Perry*, following a good Distance behind his Brother *John*, pulling a Clout out of his Pocket, dropped a Ball of Inkle,[1] which one of his Guard taking up, he desired him to restore, saying, It was only his Wife's Hair-lace; but the Party opening of it, and finding a Slip-knot at the End, went and shewed it unto *John*, who was then a good Distance before, and knew nothing of the Dropping and Taking up of this Inkle; but being shewed it, and asked, whether he knew it, shook his Head and said, Yea, to his Sorrow, for that was the String his Brother strangled his Master with. This was sworn upon the Evidence at their Trial.

The Morrow being the Lord's-day, they remained at Campden, where the Minister of the Place designing to speak to them (if possible to persuade them to Repentance, and a further Confession) they were brought to Church;[2] and in their Way thither, passing by *Richard*'s House, two of his Children meeting him, he took the lesser in his Arms, leading the other in his Hand; when, on a sudden, both their Noses fell a bleeding, which was looked upon as ominous.

Here it will be no impertinent Digression, to tell how the

[1] The name 'inkle' is still not entirely obsolete, but it does not seem pos-sible to define it more closely than to say that it was a kind of linen tape.

[2] We hear nothing further of the vicar, William Bartholomew, and, as he died on 11 Oct. in the same year, he may have taken no further part in these events.

year before Mr. Harrison had his House broken open, between Eleven and Twelve of the Clock at Noon, upon Campden Market-day, while himself and his whole Family[1] were at the Lecture;[2] a Ladder being set up to a window of the second[3] Story, and an iron Bar wrenched thence with a Ploughshare, which was left in the Room, and Seven-score Pounds in Money carried away, the Authors of which Robbery could never be found.

After this, and not many Weeks before Mr. Harrison's Absence, his Servant Perry, one Evening, in Campden-Garden made an hideous Out-cry; whereat, some who heard it, coming in, met him running, and seemingly frighted, with a Sheep-pick[4] in his Hand, to whom he told a formal Story,[5] how he had been set upon by two Men in white, with naked Swords, and how he defended himself with his Sheep-pick; the Handle whereof was cut in two or three Places, and likewise a Key in his Pocket, which he said, was done with one of their Swords.

These Passages the Justice of Peace having before heard, and calling to mind, upon *Perry*'s Confession, asked him first concerning the Robbery, when his Master lost Seven-score Pounds, out of his House, at Noon-day: Whether he knew who did it? Who answered, Yes, it was his Brother. And being further asked, Whether he were then with him? He answered No, he was then at Church; but that he gave him Notice of the Money, and told him in which Room it was, and where he might have a Ladder that would reach

---

[1] 'Family' in the sense of 'household', which would include servants.
[2] 'Lecture' in the sense of 'sermon'.
[3] Most likely what we in England now call the first floor.
[4] A pitch-fork or sheppeck, for pitching hay.
[5] What we should call a circumstantial story.

the Window; and that his Brother after told him he had the Money, and had buried it in his Garden, and that they were, at Michaelmas next, to have divided it; whereupon Search was made in the Garden, but no Money could be there found.

And being further asked concerning that other Passage of his being assaulted in the Garden; he confessed it was all a Fiction, and that, having a Design to rob his Master, he did it, that, Rogues being believed to haunt the Place, when his Master was robbed, they might be thought to have done it.

At the next Assizes, which were held in *September* following, *John*, *Joan*, and *Richard Perry* had two Indictments found against them; one for breaking into William Harrison's House, and robbing him of One-hundred and forty Pounds, in the Year 1659; the other for robbing and murdering of the said William Harrison, the Sixteenth Day of August, 1660. Upon the last Indictment, the then Judge of Assizes, Sir C. T.[1] would not try them, because the Body was not found; but they were then tried upon the other Indictment for Robbery, to which they pleaded, Not guilty; but, some whispering behind them, they soon after pleaded Guilty, humbly begging the Benefit of his Majesty's gracious Pardon, and Act of Oblivion, which was granted them.[2]

But though they pleaded Guilty to this Indictment, being thereunto prompted, as in probable, by some who were unwilling to lose Time, and trouble the Court with their Trial, in regard the Act of Oblivion pardoned them; yet they all

[1] Identified as Sir Christopher Turnor by Anthony Wood; E. Foss, *Judges of England*, vii (1864), 176 makes the identification independently and describes Turnor as 'quiet and unpretending'.

[2] For the Act of Indemnity for crimes committed before the Restoration of King Charles II see below, p. 89, n. 1.

afterwards, and at their Deaths, denied that they were guilty of that Robbery, or that they knew who did it.

Yet at this Assize, as several credible Persons have affirmed, *John Perry* still persisted in his Story, that his Mother and Brother had murdered his Master; and further added, that they had attempted to poison him in the Jail, so that he durst not eat nor drink with them.

At the next Assizes, which were the Spring following, John, Joan, and Richard Perry were, by the then Judge of Assize, Sir B. H.[1] tried upon the Indictment of Murder, and pleaded, thereunto, severally, Not Guilty; and, when John's Confession, before the Justice, was proved,[2] Viva Voce, by several Witnesses who heard the same, he told them, he was then mad, and knew not what he said.

The other two, *Richard* and *Joan Perry*, said they were wholly innocent of what they were accused, and that they knew nothing of Mr. Harrison's Death, nor what was become of him; and *Richard* said, that his Brother had accused others, as well as him, to have murdered his Master; which the Judge bidding him prove, he said, that most of those, that had given Evidence against him, knew it; but, naming none, not any spoke of it, and so the Jury found them all three Guilty.

---

[1] The first edition has 'Sir B. H.', and there was a judge called Bennet Hoskyns, whose name has been suggested; but later editions have 'Sir R. H.' Foss, *Judges of England*, vii, extends this as Sir Robert Hyde. As will be seen from p. 78 below, Sir Robert Hyde certainly was the circuit judge at Gloucester in 1662, so the 'B. H.' of the first edition is a misprint. Hyde was the severe judge who condemned Benjamin Keach to the pillory and Brian Twyne to death. He died in 1665.

[2] In the sense that they gave evidence of its genuineness, not of the truth of the statements in it.

Some few Days after, being brought to the Place of their Execution, which was on Broadway-hill, in sight of Campden; the Mother (being reputed a Witch, and to have so bewitched her Sons, they could confess nothing, while she lived) was first executed; after which, *Richard*, being upon the Ladder, professed, as he had done all along, that he was wholly innocent of the Fact for which he was then to die, and that he knew nothing of Mr. Harrison's Death, nor what was become of him; and did, with great Earnestness, beg and beseech, his Brother, for the Satisfaction of the Whole World, and his own Conscience, to declare what he knew concerning him; but he, with a dogged and surly Carriage, told the People, he was not obliged to confess to them; yet, immediately before his Death, said he knew nothing of his Master's Death, nor what was become of him, but they might hereafter possibly hear.

For Sir T. O. *Knight.*

Honoured Sir,

In Obedience to your Commands, I give you this true Account of my being carried away beyond the Seas, my Continuance there, and Return Home. On a Thursday in the Afternoon, in the Time of Harvest, I went to Charringworth, to demand Rents due to my Lady Campden; at which Time the Tenants were busy in the Fields, and late before they came Home, which occasioned my Stay there till the close of the Evening. I expected a considerable Sum, but received only Three-and-twenty Pounds, and no more. In my Return Home, in the narrow Passage amongst Ebrington Furzes, there met me one Horseman, and said, Art thou there? And I, fearing that he would have rid over

me, struck his Horse over the Nose; whereupon he struck
at me with his Sword, several Blows, and run it into my
Side, while I, with my little Cane, made my Defence as well
as I could; at last another came behind me, run me into the
Thigh, laid hold on the Collar of my Doublet, and drew
me to a Hedge, near to the Place; then came in another:
They did not take my Money, but mounted me behind one
of them, drew my Arms about his Middle, and fastened
my Wrists together with something that had a Spring-lock,
as I conceived, by hearing it give a Snap as they put it on;
then they threw a great Cloke over me, and carried me
away: In the Night they alighted at a Hay-rick, which stood
near to a Stone-pit by a Wall-side, where they took away my
Money; about two Hours before Day, as I heard one of them
tell the other he thought it to be then, they tumbled me into
the Stone-pit; they staid, as I thought, about an Hour at the
Hay-rick, when they took Horse again; one of them bade
me come out of the Pit, I answered, they had my Money
already, and asked what they would do with me; whereupon he struck me again, drew me out, and put a great
quantity of Money into my Pockets, and mounted me
again after the same Manner; and on the *Friday*, about Sun-
setting, they brought me to a lone House upon a Heath, by
a Thicket of Bushes, where they took me down almost dead,
being sorely bruised with the Carriage of the Money. When
the Woman of the House saw that I could neither stand nor
speak, she asked them, Whether or no they had brought a
dead Man? They answered No, but a Friend that was
hurt, and they were carrying him to a Surgeon; she answered,
If they did not make Haste, their Friend would be dead
before they could bring him to one. There they laid me on

Cushions, and suffered none to come into the Room but a little Girl; there we staid all Night, they giving me some Broth and Strong-waters: In the Morning, very early, they mounted me as before, and on *Saturday* Night they brought me to a Place where were two or three Houses, in one of which I lay all Night, on Cushions, by their Bedside: On *Sunday* Morning they carried me from thence, and, about Three or Four o'clock, they brought me to a Place by the Sea-side, called Deal, where they laid me down on the Ground; and, one of them staying by me, the other two walked a little way off, to meet a Man, with whom they talked; and, in their Discourse, I heard them mention seven Pounds; after which they went away together, and about Half an Hour after returned. The Man (Whose Name, as I after heard, was Wrenshaw) said, he feared I would die before he could get me on Board; then presently they put me into a Boat, and carried me on Ship-board, where my Wounds were dressed. I remained in the Ship, as near as I could reckon, about six Weeks, in which Time I was indifferently recovered of my Wounds and Weakness. Then the Master of the Ship came and told me, and the rest who were in the same Condition, that he discovered three *Turkish* Ships; we all offered to fight in the Defence of the Ship and ourselves; but he commanded us to keep close, and said he would deal with them well enough: A little Wile after he called us up, and, when we came on the Deck, we saw two Turkish Ships close by us; into one of them we were put, and placed in a dark Hole, where how long we continued, before we landed, I know not: When we were landed, they led us two Days Journey, and put us into a great House, or Prison, where we remained four Days and an Half; and then came to us eight Men to view us, who seemed to be Officers; they called us, and examined us of our Trades and Callings, which everyone answered; one said he was a Surgeon, another that he was a Broad-cloth Weaver, and I, after two or three Demands, said I had some Skill in Physick: We three were set by, and taken by three of those eight Men that came to view us: It was my Chance to be chosen by a grave Physician of Eighty-seven Years of Age, who lived near to *Smyrna*, who had formerly been in England, and knew *Crowland* in *Lincolnshire*, which he preferred before all other Places in England: He employed me to keep his Still-house,[1] and gave me a silver Bowl, double gilt, to drink in; my Business was most in that Place; but once he set me to gather Cotton-wool, which I not doing to his Mind, he struck me down to the Ground, and after drew his Stiletto to stab me, but, I holding up my Hands to him, he gave a Stamp, and turned from me, for which I render Thanks to my Lord and Saviour Jesus Christ, who staid his Hand, and preserved me. I was there about a Year and three Quarters, and then my Master fell sick, on a Thursday, and sent for me; and, calling me as he used, by the name of Boll, told me he should die, and bade me shift for myself: He died on *Saturday* following, and I presently hastened with my Bowl to a Port, almost a Day's Journey distant; the Way to which Place I knew, having been twice there employed, by my Master, about the Carriage of his Cotton-wool: When I came thither, I addressed myself to two Men, who came out of a Ship of Hamborough, which, as they said, was bound for Portugal

---

[1] A house where distillation was carried on, not a still-room in the modern sense.

within three or four Days; I inquired of them for an English Ship, they answered there was none; I intreated them to take me into their Ship, they answered they durst not, for Fear of being discovered by the Searchers, which might occasion the Forfeiture, not only of their Goods, but also of their Lives: I was very importunate with them, but could not prevail; they left me to wait on Providence, which, at length, brought another out of the same Ship, to whom I made known my Condition, craving his Assistance for my Transportation; he made me the like Answer as the former, and was as stiff in his Denial, till the sight of my Bowl put him to a Pause: He returned to the Ship, he came back again accompanied with another Sea-man, and, for my Bowl, undertook to transport me; but told me, I must be contented to lie down in the Keel, and endure many hardships; which I was content to do, to gain my Liberty; so they took me Aboard, and placed me below in the Vessel, in a very uneasy Place, and obscured me with Boards and other Things, where I lay undiscovered, not-withstanding the strict Search that was made in the Vessel; my two Chapmen, who had my Bowl, honestly furnished me with the Victuals daily, until we arrived at Lisbon in Portugal; where, as soon as the Master had left the Ship, and was gone into the City, they left me on Shore money-less to shift for myself: I knew not what course to take, but, as Providence led me, I went up into the City, and came into a fair Street; and, being weary, I turned my Back to a Wall, and leaned upon my Staff; over against me were four Gentlemen discoursing together; after a While, one of them came to me, and spoke to me in a Language that I under-stood not. I told him I was an Englishman, and understood not what he spoke; he answered me, in plain English, that he understood me, and was himself born near *Wisbeech* in *Lincolnshire*; then I related to him my sad Condition, and he, taking Compassion on me, took me with him, provided for me Lodging and Diet, and, by his Interest with a Master of a Ship bound for England, procured my Passage; and bringing me on Shipboard, he bestowed Wine and Strong-waters on me, and, at his Return, gave me eight Stivers,[1] and recommended me to the Care of the Master of the Ship, who landed me safe at Dover, from whence I made Shift to get to *London*, where being furnished with Necessaries, I came into the Country.

Thus, honoured Sir, I have given you a true Account of my great Sufferings, and happy Deliverance, by the Mercy and Goodness of God, my most Gracious Father in *Jesus Christ*, my Saviour and Redeemer; to whose Name be ascribed all Honour, Praise, and Glory. I conclude and rest

Your Worship's

in all dutiful respect,

WILLIAM HARRISON.

Sir, It has not been any Forgetfulness in me, you have no sooner heard from me; but my unhappy Distemper seizing on my right Hand, soon after my Coming down into the Country, so that till now I have been wholly deprived the Use of it. I have herewith sent you a short Narrative of that no less strange, than unhappy Business, which some Years since happened in my Neighbourhood; the Truth of every Particular whereof I am able to attest, and I think it may very well be reckoned amongst the most remarkable

[1] Perhaps eightpence, perhaps eight trifling coins.

Occurences of this Age: You may dispose of it as you please, and, in whatever else I can serve you, you may freely command me, as, Sir,

Your most affectionate Kinsman,

Burton, Aug. 23,   and humble Servant,

1676.   THO. OVERBURY.

Many question the Truth of this Account Mr. Harrison gives of himself, and his Transportation, believing he was never out of England: But there is no Question of Perry's telling a formal false Story to hang himself, his Mother, and his Brother: And since this, of which we are assured, is no less incredible than that of which we doubt; it may induce us to suspend hard Thoughts of Mr. *Harrison*, till Time, the great Discoverer of Truth, shall bring to Light this dark and mysterious Business. That Mr. *Harrison* was absent from his Habitation, Employment, and Relations, near Two Years, is certain; and, if not carried away (as he affirms) no probable Reason can be given for his Absence; he living plentifully and happily in the Service of that honourable Family, to which he had been then related above fifty Years, with the Reputation of a just and faithful Servant; and, having all his Days been a Man of sober Life and Conversa- tion, cannot now reasonably be thought in his old Age, so far, to have misbehaved himself, as in such a Manner voluntarily to have forsaken his Wife, his Children, and his Stewardship, and to leave behind him, as he then did, a considerable Sum of his Lady's Money in his House; we cannot, therefore, in Reason or Charity, but believe that Mr. *Harrison* was forcibly carried away; but by whom, or by whose Procurement, is the Question. Those, who he affirms did it, he withal affirms never before to have seen; and that he saw not his Servant *Perry*, nor his Mother, nor his Brother, the Evening he was carried away; that he was spirited, as some are said to have been,[1] is no Ways prob-able, in Respect he was an old and infirm Man, and taken from the most Inland part of the Nation; and if sold, as him-self apprehends he was, for seven Pounds, would not recom-pense the Trouble and Charge of his Conveyance to the Sea-side.

Some, therefore, have had hard Thoughts of his eldest Son, not knowing whom else to suspect; and believe the Hopes of the Stewardship, which he afterwards, by the Lord Campden's Favour, enjoyed,[2] might induce him to contrive his Father's Removal; and this they are the more confirmed in, from his Misbehaviour in it; but, on the other Side, it is hard to think the Son should be knowing of his Father's Transportation; and consequently, of these un-happy Persons Innocency, as to the Murder of him, and yet prosecute them to the Death, as he did; and, when con-demned, should be the Occasion of their being conveyed above Twenty Miles, to Suffer near *Campden*, and to pro-cure *John Perry* to be there hanged in Chains, where he might daily see him; and himself to stand at the Foot of the Ladder, when they were all executed, as likewise he did.

These Considerations, as they make it improbable the Son should be privy to his Father's Transportation, so they render the whole Matter the more dark and mysterious,

[1] That is, kidnapped for transportation overseas.

[2] As Julian, Lady Campden, William Harrison's employer, was still alive when this was published in 1676 the statement here appears to mean that by the favour of her son, the third Viscount Campden, Edward Harrison was appointed her steward.

which we must therefore leave unto him, who alone knoweth all Things, in his due Time to reveal and bring to light.

ONE of the most assiduous collectors of miscellaneous
information in the England of Charles II was the
Oxford antiquary Anthony Wood. He duly obtained a
copy of Overbury's quarto and on the blank leaves at the
end he wrote the following notes:

John Perry hung in chains on the same gallows. Richard and Joan
Perry were after execution taken down and buried under the gallows.
Three days after a gentle-woman pretending to understand witches
hired a man to dig up the grave that she might search Joan's body—
she being on horseback drew up to the grave which was opened but
the horse, starting at the sight of the body in the grave, ran away under
the gallows and her head hitting against John's feet struck her off
from the horse into the grave.

After Harrison's return John was taken down and buried and
Harrison's wife soon after (being a snotty[1] covetuous presbyterian)
hung herself in her own house—why the reader is to judge.

Upon Harrison's return to London, Sir R. Hyde was at Gloucester
in his circuit and one that had seen H. there brought the news to
Gloucester, which coming to the Hearinge of Hyde he became somewhat passionate and commanding his servant to call the messenger,
chid him for bringing false news and commanded the jailer to commit
him to prison.

These notes give no help towards solving the puzzles, nor
does another note, more promising at first sight, in another
edition of the pamphlet also in the Bodleian. Attached to
this is a letter to John Gough, another antiquary, dated
1780 and stating that the note was written by Mr. Barnsley

[1] The *Oxford English Dictionary* gives 'dirty, mean, paltry, contemptible'.

of Charringworth. Mr. Barnsley, says the letter, was a learned, sensible man'; but he seems to have been a contemporary of the writer. The edition in which his notes were written was not published until the reign of Queen Anne. They cannot be regarded as having any real evidential value; but they have been much used by modern writers and so we give them here:

Mr. Harrison's wife fell into a deep melancholy and at last hanged herself after the return of her husband; after her death there was found a letter in her scrutore[1] which she had received from her husband, dated before the execution of Joan and her two sons. There was a report that Joan had bewitched a woman that lay bedridden several years who upon her execution got up and recovered her former state of health.

We might have expected some mention of the case in a celebrated book by a Gloucestershire man, Sir Matthew Hale's *Pleas of the Crown*. This has been called a 'brief and inaccurate digest of the criminal law', but it went through seven editions. Although it was not published until 1678 it was written earlier, and perhaps much earlier, for Hale died on Christmas Day 1676 and his health was failing for some time before. He was lord chief justice of the king's bench, and on one occasion he condemned two women to death for witchcraft, saying in his summing-up that he 'made no doubt at all' of the existence of witches as proved by the Scriptures, by the laws of all nations and by the wisdom of parliament.[2] His country home at Alderley was at the other end of the county from Campden but near enough to Gloucester for gossip, especially gossip about criminal trials, to reach it from there. The book, as we shall

[1] For 'escritoire'.   [2] Cobbett, *State Trials*, vi. 687–702.

see, actually considers the problem of how to deal with a charge of murder when there is no corpse. That it does not mention this particular trial may be surprising, but it does not prove that Sir Matthew Hale never heard the story, still less that he did not think it worth discussing.

Nothing, indeed, in the way of comment can be found until the year 1689, but then we do find one from a very able and successful lawyer who most probably heard the case discussed within a year or two of its occurring. This interesting comment is in the *Remarks upon the Trials of Edward Fitzharris and others* (including Henry Cornish) pub' lished in London in 1689 by John Hawles afterwards solicitor'general to William III.

Sir John Hawles was born in 1645 and entered Queen's College, Oxford, in 1662. William Harrison would then have returned to Campden a year or two before Hawles was called to the bar, and that extraordinary case would prob' ably have been a very common subject of conversation among the law students, the bench, and the bar.

In reference to the risk of convictions on insufficient evidence he mentions the case of Joan Perry and her two sons in these terms:

To give some instances of many, it is remembered in our time where persons were convicted of the murder of a person absent, but not dead, barely by inferences upon the evidence of foolish words and actions: but the Judge before whom it was tried,[1] was so unsatisfied in the matter, because the body of the person supposed to be murdered was not to be found, that he reprieved the persons condemned; yet in a circuit afterwards, a certain unwary judge,[2] without inquiring into the reasons of the reprieve, ordered execution, and the persons to

[1] Sir Christopher Turnor.   [2] Sir R. Hyde.

be hanged in chains, which was done accordingly; and afterwards to his reproach, the person supposed to be murdered appeared alive.

The writer then referred to the earlier case related by Coke where an uncle was executed for the supposed murder of his niece who afterwards appeared and claimed her estate.[1]

[1] See below, p. 92. This paragraph and the two which precede it were written by Lord Maugham.

JOHN PAGET
1860

ALTHOUGH Hawles's comment was in print and the other scraps which we have reproduced were available for anyone who chanced to look for them, the earlier writers who tried to unravel the mystery relied, as we have said, altogether on Overbury. The first of them whom we need to notice was a man of law, John Paget, whose essay appeared in *Blackwood's Magazine* for July 1860. Paget was an acute historical critic. His most valuable historical work was in exposing certain errors in Macaulay's *History of England*, the greatest English historical publication of his time. In the nineteen-thirties Mr. Winston Churchill in his *Marlborough* set out to vindicate his hero against some charges which Macaulay made. 'The sprightly Paget' supplied him with ammunition, and he wrote a page of introduction to a new edition of the book in which Paget had first collected his papers on Macaulay.[1]

In dealing with this mystery Paget is not sprightly, but wise and serious. No doubt he enjoyed exercising his critical faculty, but he did not hunt out difficulties in order to solve

[1] *The New Examen*, 1861 and 1934.

them. Compared with later writers he shows little interest in detail. He does not concern himself with the question of what became of William Harrison during his absence, and is content to deal with the other, though perhaps connected, question of what possessed John Perry to make and persist in his false confession. Even here he does not extract a solution from the evidence. His readers might well have found such an argument tedious: the days of the English detective story had not yet come. Paget's essay has the leisurely manner of the time, and it begins with some genial local colour which may well seem old-fashioned now. Its strength lies in the combination of legal experience with a trained, but not scientifically psychological, insight into human nature, an insight which reads but does not pretend to explain its 'darkest pages'.

THE CAMPDEN WONDER[1]

THE little market-town of Chipping-Campden lies on the verge of the Cotswold Hills. It is a quaint old place, formed of one straggling street of low-gabled houses, with an ancient market-house in the middle. The ruins of Campden House, built in the year 1612 by Sir Baptist Hickes (the princely merchant who erected Hickes's Hall, and gave it to the county of Middlesex), remain a monument of the loyalty of his grandson, Baptist Lord Noel, who burnt his magnificent mansion to prevent it from falling into the hands of the Parliament troops.

Railroads have only lately traversed this out-of-the-way part of England. It is not on the highroad to anywhere, and

[1] John Paget, *Paradoxes and Puzzles: Historical, Judicial, and Literary* (1874).

though the country around possesses beauties peculiarly its own, it has never been frequented by tourists. It is best known by the love which Shakespeare evidently bore to it. There can be no doubt that it was the haunt of his boyhood. When Slender taunts Master Page by telling him that he hears his 'fallow greyhound was outrun on Cotswold', we may be sure that many a course on those wide and then open downs must have risen to Shakespeare's recollection. It is here, too, that he places that pleasant arbour in Justice Shallow's orchard, where he ate 'a last year's pippen of his own graffing with a dish of carraways, and so forth', with Falstaff and his 'cousin Silence'. It was 'a goodly dwelling and a rich'. Cousin Silence was, we have no doubt, a Campden man, and trolled out his fragments of carols at the little bowlinggreen there. Shakespeare tells us that he was a townsman. 'Is old Double of your town living yet?' Old Double, who is immortal because he died. 'See, see!—he drew a good bow. And dead!—he shot a fine shoot. John of Gaunt loved him well, and betted much money on his head. Dead! How a score of good ewes now? And is old Double dead?'

He probably acquired the skill as an archer, which endeared him to 'John of Gaunt', at those games on Dover's Hill, in the immediate neighbourhood, which were celebrated by Ben Jonson, and which were held there annually until a few years ago. 'Will Squele', too, was a 'Cotswold man'. Shakespeare must have loved the place, or he would never have coined so endearing a name. Who has not a kindly feeling towards Will Squele? The commentators have puzzled themselves greatly after their usual fashion, and have devised ingenious and improbable reasons why

Falstaff's tailor should be one 'Master Dombledon'. They have sought for abstruse meanings in the name, stupidly fancy/ ing that it was originally written Doubledone, and implied a double charge. It is simply the name of a hill a few miles beyond Campden, and the use of it affords an additional proof of Shakespeare's familiarity with the country.

This little town was, in the year 1660, the scene of a tragedy so extraordinary that it is still remembered by the name of 'The Campden Wonder'.

[Here follows a summary of Overbury's pamphlet, ending with Harrison's statement in full.]

It is difficult to say what amount of credence should be given to this extraordinary narrative. On the one hand it appears impossible to assign a sufficient motive for kid/ napping the old man. The persons who attacked him would have been exposed to far less danger of detection had they either murdered him at once, or left him to take his chance of life in the stone pit after the robbery; and much profit was not likely to accrue from the sale of the old man as a slave. On the other hand, it must be remembered that the country was at that time in a disturbed state, and that the risk of detection must not be estimated by what it would be at the present day; that kidnapping was not an uncommon crime; and that no other mode of accounting for Harrison's dis/ appearance has ever been suggested. But be this story true or not, the fact that he had not been murdered is unquestion/ able. The innocence of the Perrys of the crime for which they suffered death was established beyond the possibility of doubt; and we have to deal with the fact, a startling one certainly, that John Perry not only sacrificed the lives of two persons with whom he was closely connected, but his own also,

to a falsehood which he had no motive whatever for committing.

This opens one of the darkest and strangest pages in the
history of human nature. There can be no doubt that he was
a victim of that remarkable form of mental disease which
induces the sufferer to charge himself and others with
imaginary crimes—a malady far more common than ordinary observers suppose. From the earliest periods as to
which we have any records down to the present day, this
terrible disease has from time to time presented itself under
various forms. The purest minds and the highest intellects
have suffered from it no less than the ignorant and the de-
graded. Indeed, it would seem as if those minds which are
most delicately strung, and tuned to the most refined
sensibility, are peculiarly liable to its attack. Few men
probably have led so pure and innocent a life, or one which
afforded so little ground for self-reproval, as the poet
Cowper; yet he has told us that 'the sense of sin and the
expectation of punishment', the 'feeling that he had committed a crime'—he knew not what—was ever present to
his mind.

There is one incident of this disease, with regard to which
those who (as has been the case with ourselves in more
instances than one) are brought into contact with the sufferer
should be especially upon their guard. So thoroughly is he
convinced of the truth of his story, he narrates it with such
earnestness and simplicity, that unless some circumstance
has occurred to put the listener upon his guard, it is next to
impossible for him to refuse his assent to its truth. As one,
who has left a record of the impressions produced on his
own mind during the prevalence of delusion, has told us,

'of the two, the appearance of the bed, walls, and furniture of his room was false, not his preternatural impressions',[1] it follows, from this strong internal conviction, that nothing surprises or startles the sufferers. When John Perry was shown the cord which fell from his brother's pocket, had he been fabricating a story he would have paused to consider what he should say, and would very probably have been betrayed into a contradiction or an inconsistency. But his diseased imagination at once seized upon the circumstance as food for the delusion with which his mind was impressed, and wove it into the narrative in a manner which bore the closest possible resemblance to actual truth, because to his mind it was truth.

A case which, in some of its features, bore a striking resemblance to that of the Perrys, is recorded as having happened in the neighbourhood of Calais, nearly a century earlier.

A woman disappeared, and suspicion arose that she had been made away with. A man was found lurking in a wood in the neighbourhood, and, betraying symptoms of fear and apprehension, he was arrested on suspicion of having murdered her, confessed the crime, and was executed. In two years the woman returned. The heir of the unhappy sufferer sued the judge who had condemned him for damages. They ought not, it was argued, to have condemned any one for the murder until the body had been found, or its absence satisfactorily accounted for; in other words until the corpus delicti had been proved[2]—a principle well known to our law, and acted upon, in the first instance, in the case of the

---

[1] Narrative of the Treatment of a Gentleman during Derangement, 63, 1838.   [2] Annaeus Robertus, lib. 1, c. iv.

Perrys, whom Sir Christopher Turner refused to try at the
assizes immediately following their apprehension, on this
very ground. How the difficulty was got over afterwards does
not appear.

It is like calling up spirits from the dead to open the
stained and faded pages of the old reporters of the proceedings
in the Parliament of Paris, or the equally interesting records
of trials in our own country, and to read the harangues of
forgotten advocates upon interests long gone by, passions
long burnt out, and superstitions which the world has out-
grown. Nothing is more curious and interesting than to note
how, through each change of circumstance and opinion
the human mind remains the same, and to observe the mode
in which its delusions shape and accommodate themselves
to the prevailing belief of the day, or the particular circumstances by which the patient is surrounded.

In the year 1662, the parish of Aulderne, about midway
between Cawdor and Forres (the scene of Macbeth's interview with the witches), witnessed a very remarkable display
of the former kind. 'Master Harie Forbes' the minister of the
parish, William Dallas the Sheriff-Depute, and the other
magnates of the neighbourhood, assembled to receive the
full and voluntary confession of Isabell Gowdie. This confession is perhaps the most curious document that is to be
found relating to the history of witchcraft. We certainly
know of none that is so comprehensive. It is a compendium
of the learning on that very curious subject, and it is especially
valuable for the internal evidence which it contains, that it
was voluntary and sincere: so minute, particular, and earnest
is it, that even now it is difficult to keep in mind that it was
merely the creation of a diseased brain.

Isabell first met the devil accidentally between the farm-
lands of Drumdewin and the sea-shore, but he prevailed
upon her to give him an assignation at night in the kirk of
Alderne. There they met, Isabell being accompanied by a
confidant, one Margaret Brodie. The devil mounted the
reader's desk with a black book in his hand. Isabell re-
nounced her baptism, and putting one hand on top of her
head, and the other on the sole of her foot, made over all
between them to the arch-enemy, who thereupon baptised
her afresh in his own name. Nothing more occurred at this
interview, but it was not long before a second took place,
the details of which we must pass over. Isabell was now
wholly given up to the devil, and she and her neighbours
were employed by him in the commission of crimes of
different kinds, up to murder itself. She enumerates those
who constituted her company or 'covin', to use the technical
name; and, curiously enough, the truth of her confession is
confirmed by one at least of her supposed accomplices.
There is a wild and picturesque imagination about Isabell
Gowdie's confessions, which is not often found in such
details. When she describes the mode that was adopted to
take away the fruit of the land, she rivals the grotesque power
of Callot.

'Before Candlemas', she says, 'we went by East Kinloss,
and then we yoked a plewghe of paddokis.[1] The divill held
the plewghe, and John Younge in Mebestone, our officer,
did drywe the plewghe. Paddokis did draw the plewghe as
oxen; quickens[2] were somes;[3] a riglan's[4] horne was a
cowter; and a piece of a riglan's horn was a sok. We went
two several times about; and all we of the covin went still

---

[1] Frogs.   [2] Twitch, couchgrass.   [3] Traces.   [4] A ridgel ram.

up and downe with the plewghe praying to the divill for the fruit of that land, and that thistles and briers might grow there.'

She visited Fairyland, like Thomas the Rhymer. The Queen of Faerie was 'brawli clothed in whyte linens', and the King of Faerie was a 'braw man, weill favoured and broad faced', but she was 'affrighted by the elf bulls, which went up and downe thair rowtting and skoylling'; and her information as to that terra incognita is but scanty.

Isabell's confession occupied four days: she gives at length the uncouth rhymes by means of which tempests were raised, which enabled her to fly through the air on storms, to change her form for that of a bird, a cat, a hare, or any other animal at will. Her amours with the devil she details with marvellous particularity, and recounts one by one the murders she had committed at his instigation, when she breaks out into this passionate exclamation: 'Alace! I deserve not to be sitting hier, for I have done so manie evill deedis, especially killing of men, I deserve to be rievin upon irin harrowes, and worse if it could be devisit!' To the horror of 'Master Harie Forbes', he was himself the subject of these terrible incantations. His life was attempted several times.

'Margaret Brodie shot at Mr. Harie Forbes at the standing stanes, bot she missed, and speirit 'if she should shoot again?' And the devil said, 'Not! for we wold nocht get his lyfe at that tyme.' We intentit several tymes for him qhan he was seik. Bessie Hay, Jean Martin the maiden, Bessie Wilson, Margaret Brodie, Elspeth Neshie, and I myself, met in Bessie Wilsones hows, and maid a bag against him. The bag was maid of the flesh, guttis and gallis of toadis, the liewer of an hear, pickles of corn, and pairingis of naillis of fingers and toes. We steepit all night among water. The divill learned us to saye the wordis following at the making of the bag:—

'"He is lying on his bedd, and he is seik and sair,
Let him ly intil that bedd monethes two and dayes thrie mair.
He sal ly intill his bedd, he sal be seik and sair,
He sal ly intill his bedd monethes two and days thrie mair."

And quhan we haid said thes wordis, we wer al on our kneyis, our hair abowt our shoulderis and eyes, holding up our handis to the divill that it might destroy the said Mr. Harie. It was intendit that we, coming into his chalmer in the night-tym, sould swing it on him. And becaus we prevailed not at that tym, Bessie Hay undertook and cam into his chalmer to wisit him, being werie intimat with him, and she brought in of the bag in her handis full of the oil thereof, to have swowng and casten droppis of it on him; bot there were some uther worthie persons with him at the tym, by quhich God prevented Bessie Hay that she gat no harm don to him, bot swang a litl of it on the bed quhair he lay.'[1]

The confessions conclude with a minute account of making the image of a child of clay: 'It wanted no mark of the imag of a bairn, eyes, nose, mouth, litle lippes, and hands of it folded down by its sydis.'

Whilst the clay which formed the image was kneaded, the devil sat on a black 'kist', and Isabell and her companions chanted the following rhyme:—

'We put this water among this meall,
For long dwyning and ill heall;

[1] Isabell Gowdie's fourth confession.

> We put it intill the fyr,
> To burn them up both stik and stour,
> That be burnt with our will,
> As onie stikill on an kill.'

This image represented the child of the Laird of Parkis, 'As it was rosted eche other day at the fyr, som tymes on pairt of it, somtymes another, the bairn would be burnt and rosten, even as it was.'—'Each day we wold water it, and then rost and bak it, and turn it at the fyr, each other day, till that bairn died, and then lay it up, and steired it not untill the next bairn was borne; and then within half an yeir efter that bairne was borne, we would take it out of the cradle, and bak it and rost it at the fyr, until that bairn died also.'[1]

'All this and a great manie mor terrible thingis the said witnesses and notar heard the said Isabell confes, and most willingly and penitently speak furth of her own mouth.'

The record is imperfect, but there seems no reason to doubt that Isabell Gowdie and Janet Breadheid suffered at the stake.

The conviction of guilt was impressed upon their minds as vividly as it was upon that of John Perry, nor can we wonder at the eagerness with which Master Harie Forbes and his confederates pursued these unhappy women to the death. Sir George Mackenzie observes, that in these cases 'the accusers are masters or neighbours who had their children dead, and are engaged by grief to suspect these poor creatures. I knew [he says] one burnt because a lady was jealous of her with her husband; and the crime is so

[1] Confession of Janet Breadheid. See Pitcairn's *Criminal Trials*, III, App. vii.

odious that they are never assisted or defended by their relations. The witnesses and assizes are afraid that if they escape they will die for it, and therefore they take an unwarrantable latitude. And I have observed that scarce ever any who were accused before a country assize of neighbours did escape that trial.'[1]

We are past the age for belief in witchcraft, but the diseased imagination which formerly manifested itself in the wild delusions of poor Isabell Gowdie, now forms for itself a creation far more dangerous, because its phantoms are reconcilable with the ordinary experience of the world. Within the last two years the courts at Westminster were occupied for many days in the investigation of a charge of a most serious nature, brought against a physician by the husband of one of his patients.[2] The lady kept a journal, in which she noted down with the utmost minuteness the rise, progress, and entire history of an overwhelming and passionate attachment between herself and the doctor. This journal came to the husband's hands. The explosion may be imagined. The husband very naturally instituted proceedings for a divorce. When the trial came on, the journal, consisting of three bulky volumes, and extending over a period of five years, was produced. Nothing could be clearer, more explicit, or more astounding, than the disclosures it contained. But there was not a particle of confirmatory evidence to support any one of them; and it was established beyond a doubt that the lady, though apparently conducting herself like other people, and giving no external sign of disordered

---

[1] Mackenzie's *Works*, ii. 87.

[2] *Robinson* v. *Robinson and Lane*; Divorce Court, 14 June 1858 to 2 March 1859. See *The Times*, 6 July 1858.

intellect, was upon this particular subject altogether insane; that the doctor was innocent throughout the affair, and wholly unconscious that he had for years been made the hero of a romance rivalling the adventures of Faublas. This disease sometimes assumes a form even more dangerous than that of self-accusation. A crime is committed, or supposed to have been committed. The details of an inquiry of an exciting nature fill the columns of the press. Presently the imagination fastens upon the circumstances as they are gradually revealed, and the unfortunate patient fancies that he has been a witness of the whole transaction, comes for-ward believing that he is discharging an imperative duty, and with all the clearness, coolness, and certainty which charac-terise truth, depones to the creation of his heated brain. A case of this kind occurred at the winter assizes at Stafford, in the year 1857.

The body of a girl named Elizabeth Hopley was found in the canal at Bradley, early on the morning of the 30th of April. There were no marks of violence. About ten o'clock on the previous evening she had left the house of her aunt for the purpose of going to the place where a young man, to whom she was engaged to be married, was in the habit of working. Her road led past the place where her body was found, and it was supposed that dazzled by the light of some coke-fires, she had missed her way, and fallen over the low wall by which the canal was at that spot very insufficiently guarded. About three weeks, however, after the girl's death, a neighbour of the name of Samuel Wall declared that Elizabeth Hopley had been murdered, and that he had been present when the crime was committed. A day or two after-wards he was summoned before the magistrates, when he told the following story. He said than on the night of the 29th of April he was on duty as a private watchman on some premises near a bridge which crossed the railway; that he saw two persons, a man and a woman, on the bridge, and heard a woman's voice say, 'Philip, don't kill me! You said that you would kill me before!' That the man then raised his hand and struck the woman a violent blow on the head, which knocked her down. Upon this he went up, and instantly recognised the man as one Philip Clare, whom he well knew. He exclaimed, 'Philip, you'll have to suffer for this!' Clare turned round and replied, 'If you speak, I'll serve you the same!' Clare then lifted the young woman up from the ground, and, followed by Wall, carried her over the railway bridge, and down a road past some cottages, until he came to the canal. Here he paused, and turning round again upon Wall, said, 'Now, if you speak, or tell any one, I will kill you. I will serve you in the same way as I served her, and set some one else to watch instead.' He then, in Wall's presence, plunged the woman, who still seemed help-less and insensible, into the canal, close to the spot where, the next morning, her body was discovered.

Wall fixed the time when this occurred as twenty minutes after midnight; and it must be remarked that he was em-ployed as a watchman, and was likely to be habitually observant of time.

He said that he returned to his employer's premises, being prevented by his fear of Clare from giving any alarm; that after about a quarter of an hour had elapsed, Clare came to him and renewed his threats, when, terrified by the appre-hension of immediate violence, he locked himself up in the engine-house until daylight.

Upon this statement, Clare was taken into custody, and committed for trial. At his trial Wall repeated the story he had told the magistrates. There was a total absence of confirmation. It was met by proof that the body showed no sign of having received any blow of the kind described by Wall; that there had been men at work pumping water during the whole night in the immediate neighbourhood, who must, in all probability, have heard something, had the affair taken place as Wall described. It was shown, moreover, that from half-past six until about eleven p.m., Clare had been in a public-house at Bilston, which he left, in company with four other men, one of whom accompanied him till within half a mile of his own house. Another witness, a neighbour, proved that about twelve o'clock he met Clare, and entered into conversation with him near his own door; that they remained together until two o'clock the next morning. There could not be the slightest doubt of Clare's innocence, and the jury, of course, at once acquitted him. Nor could there be any doubt that Wall believed the story he told. The minuteness, the particularity, the graphic details, the conversation, all bear the stamp of that subjective truth, which our language has no word to distinguish from the objective truth. It is curious to observe in how many respects this case resembles that of John Perry. In both there was a period of incubation, during which the mind brooded in silence over its creations; in both the accuser professed to have been present, and thus a participant, though in different degrees, in the crime. In both the conversations with the supposed murderer are minutely detailed; in both the tale is solemnly repeated, consistently, and without variation, at considerable intervals of time, and subject to the test of judicial examination.

A case even more remarkable occurred shortly before the one we have just referred to.

A gentleman of high social position instituted proceedings against his wife with the view of obtaining a divorce.

The innocence of the lady was strongly asserted and firmly believed. Counter-charges of conspiracy and perjury were brought against the husband and his witnesses. The lady herself was in a state of disordered intellect, produced, as was asserted, by the conduct of the husband, which precluded her from taking any part, or affording any assistance towards her own defence, which, however, was vigorously maintained by friends who were firmly convinced that she was wholly innocent. The inquiry lasted for nearly four years, and at length reached the House of Lords, where the case on behalf of the husband had just terminated when Parliament rose for the Easter recess.

On the House reassembling, there appeared at the bar an elderly and respectable-looking clergyman—who, to the surprise of every one, deposed upon oath that six or seven years before—namely, in the month of May or June, in the year 1849 or '50, he could not say which—he had been an actual eyewitness of the guilt of the lady. He swore that he had never mentioned the circumstance during the six or seven years that had elapsed but to one person, and that person was dead. He had permitted his daughters and his sister to continue on terms of intimacy with the lady whom he accused. He was unable to fix the time of the occurrence, even as to the year in which it took place, or to state who was the partner in her guilt. Every avenue for contradiction was thus cut off, and the story was left to stand or fall, according as the respectable character and social position of the witness, and the apparent conviction with which he told his story, or the improbable nature of that story itself, coupled with the fact that during a most searching investiga- tion, carried on by adverse parties with the utmost eagerness for a period of between four and five years, no circumstance which in the slightest degree corroborated that story had ever come to light, might be considered to be entitled to the greater weight. It was not long, however, before the difficulty was solved. Within a few months, the witness who had given this extraordinary history gave himself up to justice, declaring with every expression of contrition that he had been guilty of forging certain bills of exchange, that they had nearly reached maturity, that he had no means of providing for them, that detection was inevitable, and that he wished to anticipate the blow, and make such reparation as was in his power by a full acknowledgement of his guilt. Upon investigation, it turned out that there was not the slightest foundation for this story; no forgery had been com- mitted—no such bills of exchange had ever been in exis- tence. His delusion as to his own guilt was as complete as his delusion as to that of the lady against whom he had given evidence, over whose strange history he had no doubt brooded for years, until the thick-coming fancies of his brain assumed the form and appearance of substantive creations.

Doctor Southwood Smith, in his 'Lectures on Forensic Medicine', after observing how common false self-inculpa- tive evidence is, gives some remarkable instances in which it has occurred. Of these the following is perhaps the most striking: 'In the war of the French Revolution the Hermione frigate was commanded by Captain Pigot, a harsh man and a severe commander. His crew mutinied, and carried the ship into an enemy's port, having murdered the captain and many of the officers under circumstances of extreme barbarity. One midshipman escaped, by whom many of the criminals, who were afterwards taken and delivered over to justice one by one, were identified. Mr. Finlaison, the Government actuary, who at that time held an official situation at the Admiralty, states: "In my own experience, I have known, on separate occasions, more than six sailors who voluntarily confessed to having struck the first blow at Captain Pigot. These men detailed all the horrid circumstances of the mutiny with extreme minuteness and perfect accuracy; nevertheless, not one of them had ever been in the ship, nor had so much as seen Captain Pigot in their lives. They had obtained, by tradition, from their messmates, the particulars of the story. When long on a foreign station, hungering and thirsting for home, their minds became enfeebled; at length they actually believed themselves guilty of the crime over which they had so long brooded, and submitted with a gloomy pleasure to being sent to England in irons for judgment. At the Admiralty we were always able to detect and establish their innocence in defiance of their own solemn asseverations." [1]

We are exhausting our space, though not the number of instances of a similar description which lie before us, and must content ourselves with one more.

A magistrate of one of the northern counties of England, well known for his active benevolence, during the discharge of his duty as one of the visiting justices of the County Lunatic Asylum, entered into conversation with one of the

[1] *London Medical Gazette*, Jan. 1838.

patients, and was much struck with his rational demeanour and sensible remarks. The man expressed himself grateful for the kindness with which he was treated, and said that he was well aware that it was necessary that he should be under restraint; that although he was perfectly well at that time, he knew that he was at any moment liable to a return of the insanity, during an attack of which he had some years before murdered his wife; and that it would be unsafe to permit him to go at large. He then expressed the deepest contrition for his crime; and after some further conversation the magistrate left him, not doubting the truth of his story. Referring to the case in conversation with the master of the asylum, he expressed much interest, and referred to the patient as 'That unhappy criminal lunatic who had murdered his wife'; when, to his astonishment, he was informed that the wife was alive and well, and had been to visit her husband only the day before!

We cannot conclude our observations on this interesting subject better than in the words of the old jurist Heineccius:[1] 'Confession is sometimes the voice of conscience. Experience, however, teaches us that it is frequently far otherwise. There sometimes lurks, under the shadow of an apparent tranquillity, an insanity which impels men readily to accuse themselves of all kinds of iniquity. Some, deluded by their imaginations, suspect themselves of crimes which they have never committed. A melancholy temperament, the taedium vitae, and an unaccountable propensity to their own destruction, urges some to the most false confessions; whilst they were extracted from others by the dread of torture, or the tedious misery of the dungeon. So far is it from

[1] Exer. 18, 6.

being the fact that all confessions are to be attributed to the stings of conscience, that it has been well said by Calpurnius Flaccus, "Even a voluntary confession is to be regarded with suspicion"; and by Quintilian, "a suspicion of insanity is inherent in the nature of all confessions".'

ANDREW LANG

1904

VERY different from Paget was Andrew Lang, who wrote a generation later; a most various, delightful, and brilliant historian, folk⁄lorist, anthropologist, poet, and man of letters. He was a story⁄teller and a lover of stories of all kinds and all ages; but he also sparkled with ideas and theories about innumerable subjects. He retold the Campden story in his own way, which was so unlike any other man's that we give his article in full.[1] The reader will perceive that Lang was a Scotsman, with a devotion to the house of Stuart; but it would be most unfair to class him as a mere purveyor of costume⁄history; he wrote more than professors write, and he wrote faster, but he did not wilfully disregard academic standards.

THE CAMPDEN MYSTERY

I

THE ordinary historical mystery is at least so far clear that one or other of two solutions must be right, if we only knew which. Perkin Warbeck was the rightful King,

[1] Originally published in the *Cornhill Magazine* in 1904, it was reprinted in *Historical Mysteries* (1904), which has been reprinted.

or he was an impostor. Giacopo Stuardo at Naples (1669) was the eldest son of Charles II., or he was a humbug. The Man in the Iron Mask was *certainly* either Mattioli or Eustache Dauger. James VI. conspired against Gowrie, or Gowrie conspired against James VI., and so on. There is reason and human nature at the back of these puzzles. But at the back of the Campden mystery there is not a glimmer of reason or of sane human nature, except on one hypothesis, which I shall offer. The occurrences are, to all appearance, motiveless as the events in a feverish dream. 'The whole Matter is dark and mysterious; which we must therefore leave unto Him who alone knoweth all Things, in His due Time, to reveal and to bring to Light.'

So says the author of 'A True and Perfect Account of the Examination, Confession, Trial, and Execution of *Joan Perry*, and her two Sons, *John* and *Richard Perry*, for the Supposed Murder of *Will Harrison*, Gent., Being One of the most remarkable Occurrences which hath happened in the Memory of Man. Sent in a Letter (by *Sir Thomas Over-bury*, of *Burton*, in the County of *Gloucester*, Knt., and one of his Majesty's Justices of the Peace) to *Thomas Shirly*, Doctor of Physick, in London. Also Mr. *Harrison's* Own account', &c. (London. Printed for John Atkinson, near the Chapter House, in *St. Paul's Church-Yard*. No date, but apparently of 1676.)

Such is the vast and breathless title of a pamphlet which, by undeserved good luck, I have just purchased. The writer, Sir Thomas Overbury, 'the nephew and heir', says Mr. John Paget, 'of the unhappy victim of the infamous Coun-tess of Somerset' (who had the elder Overbury poisoned in the Tower), was the Justice of the Peace who acted

as *Juge d'Instruction* in the case of Harrison's disappearance.[1]

To come to the story. In 1660, William Harrison, Gent.,
was steward or 'factor' to the Viscountess Campden, in
Chipping Campden, Gloucestershire, a single-streeted
town among the Cotswold hills. The lady did not live in
Campden House, whose owner burned it in the Great
Rebellion, to spite the rebels; as Castle Tirrim was burned
by its Jacobite lord in the '15. Harrison inhabited a portion
of the building which had escaped destruction. He had
been for fifty years a servant of the Hickeses and Campdens,
his age was seventy (which deepens the mystery), he was
married, and had offspring, including Edward, his eldest
son.

On a market day, in 1659, Mr. Harrison's house was
broken into, at high noon, while he and his whole family
were 'at the Lecture', in church, a Puritan form of edification.
A ladder had been placed against the wall, the bars of a
window on the second story had been wrenched away with
a ploughshare (which was left in the room), and 140*l.* of
Lady Campden's money were stolen. The robber was never
discovered—a curious fact in a small and lonely village. The
times, however, were disturbed, and a wandering Cavalier
of Roundhead soldier may have 'cracked the crib'. Not
many weeks later, Harrison's servant, Perry, was heard
crying for help in the garden. He showed a 'sheep-pick',
with a hacked handle, and declared that he had been set
upon by two men in white, with naked swords, and had
defended himself with his rustic tool. It is curious that Mr.
John Paget, a writer of great acuteness, and for many years

[1] Paget, *Paradoxes and Puzzles*, p. 342, Blackwoods, 1874.

Cambden House

CAMPDEN HOUSE

The inhabited remnant, from an eighteenth-century water-colour drawing
in the Sutherland Collection, Ashmolean Museum, Oxford

police magistrate at Hammersmith, says nothing of the robbery of 1659, and of Perry's crazy conduct in the garden.[1] Perry's behaviour there, and his hysterical invention of the two armed men in white, gave the key to his character. The two men in white were never traced, of course, but, later, we meet three men not less flagitious, and even more mysterious. They appear to have been three 'men in buckram'.

At all events, in quiet Campden, adventures obviously occurred to the unadventurous. They culminated in the following year, on August 16, 1660. Harrison left his house in the morning (?) and walked the two miles to Charringworth to collect his lady's rents. The autumn day closed in, and between eight and nine o'clock old Mrs. Harrison sent the servant, John Perry, to meet his master on the way home. Lights were also left burning in Harrison's window. That night neither master nor man returned, and it is odd that the younger Harrison, Edward, did not seek for his father till very early next morning: he had the convenience, for nocturnal search, of a moon which rose late. In the morning, Edward went out and met Perry, returning alone: he had not found his master. The pair walked to Ebrington, a village half way between Campden and Charringworth, and learned that Harrison had called, on the previous evening, as he moved home through Ebrington, at the house of one Daniel. The hour is not given, but Harrison certainly disappeared when just beyond Ebrington, within less than a mile from Campden. Edward and Perry next heard that a poor woman had picked up on the highway, beyond Ebrington, near some whins or furze, a hat,

[1] See his *Paradoxes and Puzzles*, pp. 337-70, and, for good reading, see the book *passim*.

band, and comb, which were Harrison's; they were found within about half a mile of his own house. The band was bloody, the hat and comb were hacked and cut. Please observe the precise words of Sir Thomas Overbury, the justice who took the preliminary examinations: 'The Hat and Comb being hacked and cut, and the Band bloody, but nothing more could there be found.' Therefore the hat and comb were not on Harrison's head when they were hacked and cut: otherwise they must have been blood-stained; the band worn about the throat was bloody, but there was no trace of blood on the road. This passage contains the key to the puzzle.

On hearing of the discovery of these objects all the people rushed to hunt for Harrison's corpse, which they did not find.

An old man like Harrison was not likely to stay at Charringworth very late, but it seems that whatever occurred on the highway happened after twilight.

Suspicion fell on John Perry, who was haled before the narrator, Sir Thomas Overbury, J.P. Perry said that after starting for Charringworth to seek his master on the previous evening, about 8.45 P.M., he met by the way William Reed of Campden, and explained to him that as he was timid in the dark he would go back and take Edward Harrison's horse and return. Perry did as he had said, and Reed left him 'at Mr. Harrison's Court gate'. Perry dallied there till one Pierce came past, and with Pierce (he did not say why) 'he went a bow's shot into the fields', and so back once more to Harrison's gate. He now lay for an hour in a hen house, he rose at midnight, and again—the moon having now risen and dispelled his fears—he started for Charringworth.

He lost his way in a mist, slept by the road-side, proceeded in the dawn to Charringworth, and found that Harrison had been there on the previous day. Then he came back and met Edward Harrison on his way to seek his father at Charringworth.

Perry's story is like a tale told by an idiot, but Reed, Pierce, and two men at Charringworth corroborated as far as their knowledge went. Certainly Perry had been in company with Reed and Pierce, say between nine and ten on the previous night. Now, if evil had befallen Harrison it must have been before ten at night; he would not stay so late, if sober, at Charringworth. Was he usually sober? The cool way in which his wife and son took his absence suggests that he was a late-wandering old boy. They may have expected Perry to find him in his cups and tuck him up comfortably at Charringworth or at Ebrington.

Till August 24 Perry was detained in prison, or, odd to say, at the inn! He told various tales; a tinker or a servant had murdered his master and hidden him in a bean-rick, where, on search being made, *non est inventus*. Harrison, and the rents he had collected, were vanished in the azure. Perry now declared that he would tell all to Overbury, and to no other man. To him Perry averred that his mother and brother, Joan and Richard Perry, had murdered Harrison! It was his brother who, by John Perry's advice and connivance, had robbed the house in the previous year, while John 'had a Halibi,' being at church. The brother, said John, buried the money in the garden. It was sought for, but was not found. His story of the 'two men in white,' who had previously attacked him in the garden, was a lie, he said. I may add that it was not the lie of a sane man. Perry was conspicuously crazy.

He went on with his fables. His mother and brother, he declared, had often asked him to tell them when his master went to collect rents. He had done so after Harrison started for Charringworth on the morning of August 16. John Perry next gave an account of his expedition with his brother in the evening of the fatal day, an account which was incompatible with his previous tale of his doings and with the authentic evidence of Reed and Pierce. Their honest version destroyed Perry's new falsehood. He declared that Richard Perry and he had dogged Harrison, as he came home at night, into Lady Campden's grounds; Harrison had used a key to the private gate. Richard followed him into the grounds; John Perry, after a brief stroll, joined him there and found his mother (how did she come thither?) and Richard standing over the prostrate Harrison, whom Richard incontinently strangled. They seized Harrison's money and meant to put his body 'in the great sink by Wallington's Mill'. John Perry left them, and knew not whether the body was actually thrown into the sink. In fact, *non est inventus* in the sink, any more than in the bean-rick. John next introduced his meeting with Pierce, but quite forgot that he had also met Reed, and did not account for that part of his first story, which Reed and Pierce had both corroborated. The hat, comb, and band John said that he himself had carried away from Harrison's body, had cut them with his knife, and thrown them into the highway. Whence the blood on the band came he neglected to say.

On the strength of this impossible farrago of insane falsehoods, Joan and Richard Perry were arrested and brought before Overbury. Not only the 'sink' but the Campden fish-pools and the ruinous parts of the house were vainly searched in quest of Harrison's body. On August 25 the three Perrys were examined by Overbury, and Richard and the mother denied all that John laid to their charge. John persisted in his story, and Richard admitted that he and John had spoken together on the morning of the day when Harrison vanished, 'but nothing passed between them to that purpose'.

As the three were being brought back from Overbury's house to Campden an unfortunate thing happened. John was going foremost when Richard, a good way behind, dropped 'a ball of inkle from his pocket'. One of his guards picked it up, and Richard said that it was 'only his wife's hair-lace'. At one end, however, was a slip-knot. The finder took it to John, who, being a good way in front, had not seen his brother drop it. On being shown the string John shook his head, and said that 'to his sorrow he knew it, for that was the string his brother strangled his master with'. To this circumstance John swore at the ensuing trial.

The Assizes were held in September, and the Perrys were indicted both for the robbery in 1659 and the murder in 1660. They pleaded 'Guilty' to the first charge, as some one in court whispered to them to do, for the crime was covered by the Act of Pardon and Oblivion passed by Charles II. at his happy Restoration. If they were innocent of the robbery, as probably they were, they acted foolishly in pleading guilty. We hear of no evidence against them for the robbery, except John's confession, which was evidence perhaps against John, but was none against *them*. They thus damaged their case, for if they were really guilty of the robbery from Harrison's house, they were the most likely people in the neighbourhood to have robbed him again and

murdered him. Very probably they tied the rope round their
own necks by taking advantage of the good King's indemnity. They later withdrew their confession, and probably
were innocent of the theft in 1659.

On the charge of murder they were not tried in September.
Sir Christopher Turner would not proceed 'because the
body of Harrison was not found'. There was no *corpus delicti*,
no evidence that Harrison was really dead. Meanwhile John
Perry, as if to demonstrate his lunacy, declared that his
mother and brother had tried to poison him in prison! At
the Spring Assizes in 1661, Sir B. Hyde,[1] less legal than
Sir Christopher Turner, did try the Perrys on the charge of
murder. How he could do this does not appear, for the
account of the trial is not in the Record House, and I am
unable at present to trace it. In the *Arminian Magazine*, John
Wesley publishes a story of a man who was hanged for
murdering another man, whom he afterwards met in one of
the Spanish colonies of South America. I shall not here
interrupt the tale of the Perrys by explaining how a hanged
man met a murdered man, but the anecdote proves that to
inflict capital punishment for murder without proof that
murder has been committed is not only an illegal but an
injudicious proceeding. Probably it was assumed that
Harrison, if alive, would have given signs of life in the
course of nine or ten months.

At the trial in spring all three Perrys pleaded 'not guilty'.
John's confession being proved against him, 'he told them
he was then mad and knew not what he said'. There must
have been *some* evidence against Richard. He declared that his
brother had accused others besides him. Being asked to prove

[1] For the mistake in Sir Robert Hyde's initial see above, p. 23, n. 1. G. N. C.

this, he answered 'that most of those that had given evidence against him knew it', but named none. So evidence had been given (perhaps to the effect that Richard had been flush of money), but by whom, and to what effect, we do not know.

The Perrys were probably not of the best repute. The mother, Joan, was supposed to be a witch. This charge was seldom brought against popular well-living people. How intense was the fear of witches, at that date, we know from the stories and accounts of trials in Glanvil's *Sadducismus Triumphatus*. The neighbours probably held that Joan Perry would, as a witch, be 'nane the waur o' a hanging'. She was put to death first, under the belief that any hypnotic or other unholy influence of hers, which prevented her sons from confessing, would be destroyed by her death. We are not aware that post-hypnotic suggestion is removed by the death of the suggester; the experiment has not been tried. The experiment failed in Joan's case. Poor Richard, who was hanged next, could not induce the 'dogged and surly' John to clear his character by a dying declaration. Such declarations were then held irrefragable evidence, at least in Scotland, except when (as in the case of George Sprot, hanged for the Gowrie conspiracy) it did not suit the Presbyterians to believe the dying man. When John was being turned off, he said that 'he knew nothing of his master's death, nor what was become of him, but they might hereafter (possibly) hear'. Did John know something? It would not surprise me if he had an inkling of the real state of the case.

II

They *did* hear; but what they heard, and what I have now to tell, was perfectly incredible. When 'some' years (two apparently) had passed, Will Harrison, Gent., like the three silly ewes in the folk-rhyme, 'came hirpling hame'. Where had the old man been? He explained in a letter to Sir Thomas Overbury, but his tale is as hard to believe as that of John Perry.

He states that he left his house in the afternoon (not the morning) of Thursday, August 16, 1660. He went to Charringworth to collect rents, but Lady Campden's tenants were all out harvesting. August seems an odd month for rent-collecting when one thinks of it. They came home late, which delayed Harrison 'till the close of the evening'. He only received 23*l.*, which John Perry said, at his first examination in 1660, had been paid by one Edward Plaisterer, and Plaisterer corroborated. Harrison then walked homeward, in the dusk probably, and, near Ebrington, where the road was narrow, and bordered by whins, 'there met me one horseman who said "*Art thou there?*"' Afraid of being ridden over, Harrison struck the horse on the nose, and the rider, with a sword, struck at him and stabbed him in the side. (It was at this point of the road, where the whins grew, that the cut hat and bloody band were found, but a thrust in the side would not make a neckband bloody.) Two other horsemen here came up, one of them wounded Harrison in the thigh. They did not now take his 23*l.*, but placed him behind one of them on horseback, handcuffed him, and threw a great cloak over him.

Now, is it likely that highwaymen would carry handcuffs which closed, says Harrison, with a spring and a snap? The story is pure fiction, and bad at that. Suppose that kidnapping, not robbery, was the motive (which would account for the handcuffs), what had any mortal to gain by kidnapping, for the purpose of selling him into slavery, a 'gent.' of seventy years of age?

In the night they took Harrison's money and 'tumbled me down a stone-pit'. In an hour they dragged him out again, and he naturally asked what they wanted with him, as they had his money already. One of these miscreants wounded Harrison again, and—stuffed his pockets full of 'a great quantity of money'. If they had a great quantity of money, what did they want with 23*l.*? We hear of no other robberies in the neighbourhood, of which misdeeds the money might have been the profits. And why must Harrison carry the money? (It has been suggested that, to win popular favour, they represented themselves as smugglers, and Harrison, with the money, as their gallant purser, wounded in some heroic adventure.)

They next rode till late on August 17, and then put Harrison down, bleeding and 'sorely bruised with the carriage of the money', at a lonely house. Here they gave their victim broth and brandy. On Saturday they rode all day to a house, where they slept, and on Sunday they brought Harrison to Deal, and laid him down on the ground. This was about three in the afternoon. Had they wanted to make for the sea, they would naturally have gone to the *west* coast. While one fellow watched Harrison, two met a man, and 'I heard them mention seven pounds.' The man to whom seven pounds were mentioned (Wrenshaw was his name, as Harrison afterwards heard—where?) said that he thought Harrison would die before he could be put on board a ship. *Que diable allait-il faire dans cette galère?* Harrison was, however, put on board a casual vessel, and remained in the ship for six weeks.

Where was the land to which the ship would go?
Far, far ahead is all the sailors know!

Harrison does not say into what 'foam of perilous seas, in
faery lands forlorn' the ship went wandering for six mortal
weeks. Like Lord Bateman:

He sailéd East, and he sailéd West,
Until he came to famed Turkee,
Where he was taken and put in prison,
Till of his life he was wear—ee!

'Then the Master of the ship came and told me, *and the rest
who were in the same condition*, that he discovered three Turkish
ships.' 'The rest who were in the same condition!' We are to
understand that a whole cargo of Harrisons was kidnapped
and consigned captive to a vessel launched on ocean, on the
off chance that the captain might meet three Turkish rovers
who would snap them up. At this rate of carrying on, there
must have been disappearances as strange as Harrison's,
from dozens of English parishes, in August 1660. Had a
crew of kidnappers been taking captives for purposes of
private fiscal policy, they would have shipped them to the
Virginian plantations, where Turkish galleys did not venture,
and they would not have kidnapped men of seventy. Moreover, kidnappers would not damage their captives by stab-
bing them in the side and thigh, when no resistance was
made, as was done to Harrison.

'The rest who were in the same condition' were 'dumped
down' near Smyrna, where the valuable Harrison was
sold to 'a grave physician'. 'This Turk he' was eighty-seven
years of age, and 'preferred Crowland in Lincolnshire before
all other places in England'. No inquiries are known to have

been made about a Turkish medical man who once practised at Crowland in Lincolnshire, though, if he ever did,
he was likely to be remembered in the district. This Turk
he employed Harrison in the still room, and as a hand in the
cotton fields, where he once knocked his slave down with his
fist—pretty well for a Turk of eighty-seven! He also gave
Harrison (whom he usually employed in the chemical
department of his business) 'a silver bowl, double gilt, to
drink in, and named him Boll'—his way of pronouncing
bowl—no doubt he had acquired a Lincolnshire accent.

This Turk fell ill on a Thursday, and died on Saturday,
when Harrison tramped to the nearest port, bowl and all.
Two men in a Hamburg ship refused to give him a passage,
but a third, for the price of his silver-gilt bowl, let him come
aboard. Harrison was landed, without even his bowl, at
Lisbon, where he instantly met a man from Wisbech, in
Lincolnshire. This good Samaritan gave Harrison wine,
strong waters, eight stivers, and his passage to Dover, whence
he came back to Campden, much to the amazement of
mankind. We do not hear the names of the ship and skipper
that brought Harrison from Lisbon to Dover. Wrenshaw
(the man to whom seven pounds 'were mentioned') is the
only person named in this delirious tissue of nonsense.

The editor of our pamphlet says, 'Many question the
truth of this account Mr. Harrison gives of himself, and his
transportation, believing he was never out of England.' I
do not wonder at their scepticism. Harrison had 'all his days
been a man of sober life and conversation', we are told, and
the odd thing is that he 'left behind him a considerable sum
of his Lady's money in his house'. He did not see any of the
Perrys on the night of his disappearance. The editor admits

that Harrison, as an article of merchandise, was not worth his freight to Deal, still less to Smyrna. His son, in his absence, became Lady Campden's steward, and behaved but ill in that situation. Some suspected that this son arranged the kidnapping of Harrison, but, if so, why did he secure the hanging of John Perry, in chains, on Broadway hill, 'where he might daily see him'?

That might be a blind. But young Harrison could not expect John Perry to assist him by accusing himself and his brother and mother, which was the most unlooked-for event in the world. Nor could he know that his father would come home from Charringworth on August 16, 1660, in the dark, and so arrange for three horsemen, in possession of a heavy weight of specie, to stab and carry off the aged sire. Young Harrison had not a great fardel of money to give them, and if they were already so rich, what had they to gain by taking Harrison to Deal, and putting him, with 'others in the same condition', on board a casual ship? They could have left him in the 'stone-pit': he knew not who they were, and the longer they rode by daylight, with a hatless, handcuffed, and sorely wounded prisoner, his pockets over-burdened with gold, the more risk of detection they ran. A company of three men ride, in broad daylight, through England from Gloucestershire to Deal. Behind one of them sits a wounded, *and hatless*, and handcuffed captive, his pockets bulging with money. Nobody suspects anything, no one calls the attention of a magistrate to this extraordinary *démarche!* It is too absurd!

The story told by Harrison is conspicuously and childishly false. At every baiting place, at every inn, these weird riders must have been challenged. If Harrison told truth, he must have named the ship and skipper that brought him to Dover.

Dismissing Harrison's myth, we ask, what could account for his disappearance? He certainly walked, on the evening of August 16, to within about half a mile of his house. He would not have done that had he been bent on a senile amour involving his absence from home, and had that scheme of pleasure been in his mind, he would have pro⁄vided himself with money. Again, a fit of 'ambulatory som⁄nambulism', and the emergence of a split or secondary personality with forgetfulness of his real name and address, is not likely to have seized on him at that very moment and place. If it did, as there were no railways, he could not rush off in a crowd and pass unnoticed through the country.

Once more, the theory of ambulatory somnambulism does not account for his hacked hat and bloody band found near the whins on the road beyond Ebrington. Nor does his own story account for them. He was stabbed in the side and thigh, he says. This would not cut his hat or ensanguine his band. On the other hand, he would leave pools and tracks of blood on the road—'the high way'. 'But nothing more could there be found', no pools or traces of blood on the road. It follows that the hacked hat and bloody band were a designed false trail, *not* left there by John Perry, as he falsely swore, but by some other persons.

The inference is that for some reason Harrison's presence at Campden was inconvenient to somebody. He had lived through most troubled times, and had come into a changed state of affairs with new masters. He knew some secret of the troubled times: he was a witness better out of the way. He may conceivably have held a secret that bore on the case of one of the Regicides; or that affected private interests, for he was the trusted servant of a great family. He was therefore spirited away: a trail certainly false—the cut hat and bloody band—was laid. By an amazing coincidence his servant, John Perry, went more or less mad—he was not sane on the evening of Thursday, August 16, and accused himself, his brother, and mother. Harrison was probably never very far from Campden during the two or three years of his disap/ pearance. It was obviously made worth his while to tell his absurd story on his return, and to accept the situation. No other hypothesis 'colligates the facts'. What Harrison knew, why his absence was essential, we cannot hope to discover. But he never was a captive in 'famed Turkee'. Mr. Paget writes: 'It is impossible to assign a sufficient motive for kid/ napping the old man . . . much profit was not likely to arise from the sale of the old man as a slave.' Obviously there was no profit, especially as the old man was delivered in a wounded and imperfect condition. But a motive for keeping Harrison out of the way is only hard to seek because we do not know the private history of his neighbours. Roundheads among them may have had excellent reasons, under the Restoration, for sequestering Harrison till the revenges of the Restoration were accomplished. On this view the mystery ceases to be mysterious, for such mad self/accusations as that of John Perry are not uncommon.[1]

[1] Not only have I failed to trace the records of the Assize at which the Perrys were tried, but the newspapers of 1660 seem to contain no account of the trial (as they do in the case of the Drummer of Tedworth, 1663), and Miss E. M. Thompson, who kindly undertook the search, has not even found a ballad or broadside on 'The Campden Wonder' in the British Museum. The pamphlet of 1676 has frequently been republished, in whole or in part, as in *State Trials*, xiv, in appendix to the case of Captain Green.

THE FIRST NEW EVIDENCE
1926

THE footnote at the end of Andrew Lang's article seemed to show that historians would be unable to carry out their traditional procedure of checking their narrative source by a comparison with other direct evidence. There were, however, means of testing the reliability of the only available source. All the allusions to places fitted in accurately with the topography of Campden and its neighbourhood. The time occupied by the various comings and goings showed no discrepancies. No error could be detected in the references to the four known characters in the story, Sir Thomas Overbury, the vicar, and the judges. The one public event referred to, the Act of Indemnity, was referred to correctly. There was one other fact which could be verified: according to the story the moon rose while John Perry was in the hen-roost, which he left at midnight, having been sent out to search for his master between eight and nine. There was nothing seriously wrong here either: On 16 August 1660 (Old Style) sunset occurred at about 7.03 p.m. and the moon rose at Campden at approximately 9.45 p.m.[1] And the sixteenth was, sure enough, a Thursday.

There were some more general matters which perhaps deserved examination. It will be remembered that Paget, in his Shakespearian paragraph, made the point that Camp⁄den was a town. His reason for saying so was not quite adequate, because 'town' at that date also meant a village, and Andrew Lang wrote of it as 'a small and lonely village'. The smaller it was, the more likely the inhabitants were to know of one another's doings. The more remote it was, the more ignorant they would be and the more easily misled by rumours of witchcraft. News of strange doings there would spread less quickly, and it would be easier to abscond from such a place without being detected. Although there was no national census in those days we happen to know fairly well how big Campden was: forty years or so earlier the whole parish had 1,700 inhabitants, of whom more than 1,100 were in Campden itself.[2] It enjoyed the status of a market⁄town, and it had a grammar school. It was not an isolated community of rustics. What inferences we may draw from its remoteness is harder to decide, for the effect of distance on the spread of news can only be estimated if we know a great deal about the state of society. Campden was a little more than ninety miles from London, which meant normally three days' journey on horseback, thirty or so from Glou⁄

[1] This information has been most kindly supplied by Sir Harold Spencer Jones, F.R.S., formerly Astronomer Royal, who adds: 'these are Greenwich Mean Times, though almost certainly in 1660 local time would have been kept.'

[2] R. Atkyns, *The Ancient and Present State of Gloucestershire*, 2nd edn. (1768), p. 167, which is a reprint of the 1st edition (1712). This is near enough to the estimate of 300 families (or households) in the Survey of Church Livings cited by Rushen, p. 56.

cester, twelve from Stratford-on-Avon, and nine from Evesham. There does not seem to have been a service of stagecoaches to this neighbourhood yet,[1] but the London road was frequented by clothiers and by the strings of packhorses which carried their cloth. It may well have been easy for a man of inconspicuous appearance to vanish from such a point on the map; but most probably news and rumours travelled far and fast. Here again, Harrison's statement seems if possible more fantastic than before, but there is nothing to discredit the rest of the *True and Perfect Account*.

Another line of inquiry, however, led to a more fundamental scepticism. This may be called 'form-criticism'. To the first glance the pamphlet looks spontaneous and unsophisticated. First comes the main story, then Harrison's piece, then the letter to Shirley, and finally the inconclusive conclusion. A skilful artist could have woven it all into a unified fabric. A competent literary journeyman could have begun or ended with the letter to Shirley instead of letting it interrupt the flow of the rest. Both artists and journeymen were used to handling this sort of material. The return of the wanderer is one of the ever-recurring themes of literature. In the seventeenth century many a time the wanderer returned from captivity among the Turks or Moors. Even in remote places where no neighbour had ever come back home from such a terrible experience, everyone knew that Englishmen were held as prisoners in Morocco, Algiers, Tunis, Tripoli, and farther east.[2] Even where no news had penetrated of

---

[1] See Joan Parkes, *Travel in England in the Seventeenth Century* (1925).

[2] There is no need to refer to the extensive body of information about this subject, but I wish to draw attention to a recent book which sets it in a new light, Sir Godfrey Fisher's absorbing *Barbary Legend* (1957).

Admiral Blake's expedition to the Mediterranean in 1655, the villagers had heard 'briefs' read out in church calling on them to contribute money for the ransoms of these slaves. Captivity among the Mahommedans was not only a common fact; it was a familiar theme in fiction. It was a convenient device for an author who wanted one of his characters to be temporarily out of the way and to return, perhaps to spin a story within the story. To mention only very famous books, it appears in *Don Quixote*, in *l'Avare*, and in *Robinson Crusoe*.

With a little ingenuity we could suggest reasons why a liar in Campden should bring in Smyrna, cotton-growing, and some of the other details of this captivity-story; but a much more exciting perspective opens. Is not the whole pamphlet, with its story within the story, a work of fiction? Has not the writer distracted our attention from the im-probabilities of his story about Harrison's disappearance by the far wilder improbabilities of the story which he makes Harrison tell? This, after all, is a conjuring trick which other writers have pulled off, and so have clever deceivers in real life. If Sir Thomas Overbury did it, he was a deceiver of a very high order, with his scrupulous care for detail and his feigned *naïveté*; but this solution cuts all the knots. It relieves us from any further perplexity about Harrison's movements or Perry's motives.

The present editor confesses, with compunction which does not, however, amount to shame, that this was his own opinion so long as he knew of no other authority than the *True and Perfect Account*. A writer of detective-stories who stands high in that craft reached a similar conclusion on different grounds. Mr. E. R. Punshon wrote: 'What probably did happen was that in the district there was vague gossip about the dead man having been seen somewhere, and that our unknown pamphleteer saw his chance to invent a sensational story and launch it on the world—very successfully.'[1] By the time when Mr. Punshon wrote, a new authority had been discovered for one main part of the story, and Mr. Punshon therefore does not reject the whole story from beginning to end. He does not believe in the return of Harrison, but he accepts the trials and executions. We must now go back to Andrew Lang's footnote. Miss E. M. Thompson had searched for further printed evidence in the most appropriate places, but unsuccessfully, and this absence of confirmation was the strongest count against Overbury. The interval of fourteen years from the events to the publication of his pamphlet was another. In 1926, however, a distinguished medical authority, Sir John Collie, read a paper on the mystery to the MedicoLegal Society.[2] During the discussion which followed an eminent lawyer, Lord Justice Atkin, as he then was, spoke as follows: 'He had found, at the Record Office, the book of the Clerk of Assize of the Oxford circuit for the period in question. Unfortunately there were no entries for the Summer circuit of 1660, although blank spaces have been left for them. This was possibly due to the fact that it was the first circuit after the Restoration, and there may have been a vacancy in the office of Clerk of Assize. For the Assize of 1661, the entries were complete, and the narrative of the pamphlet was fully confirmed, so far as the trial and conviction of the Perrys were concerned. There was an entry that the

---

[1] Letter to *The Times Literary Supplement*, 4 Dec. 1948.
[2] *Transactions of the MedicoLegal Society*, xx (1926).

three were indicted for the murder of Harrison, pleaded not guilty,[1] were convicted, and there was the ominous entry "sus."'

The following is from the record of the jail delivery at Gloucester on Wednesday, 3 March, 13 Charles II, before Robert Hyde, one of the justices of the bench and justice of jail delivery.[2]

Posuit se culpabilem.

[3]SS[r] Judicium. Johannes Perrey pro murdro per inter-
feccionem Wilhelmi Harrison generosi
apud Chipping Campden

Posuit se culpabilem.

[3]Ss[r] Judicium. Ricardus Perrey pro eodem.

Posuit se culpabilem.

[3]Ss[r] Judicium. Johanna Perrey pro eodem.

This may be translated in one sentence: John, Richard, and Joan Perry pleaded guilty to the murder of William Harri-son, gentleman, and were sentenced to be hanged. Whether the record also states that they were then hanged is not certain; but as the fact of the sentence is established, there

[1] As will be seen from the extract printed below, 'not guilty' is a slip of the pen.

[2] Assizes 2/1. I am much indebted to Mr. C. T. Flower, formerly deputy keeper of the public records, who provided this transcript and caused a search for the indictment to be made in Assizes 5/1. These records were at the time at Belvoir Castle.

[3] The assistant keeper of the public records who transcribed the passage, a very experienced reader, was unable to say definitely whether this con-traction was SS[r] (let him be hanged) or S[s] (hanged). Mr. Flower thought the latter the more likely. The other contractions, jud', and po' se cul', pre-sented no difficulty.

can no longer be any reason for doubting that Overbury and Hawles were right in believing this too. This was the stage in the clearing-up of the mystery which had been reached when Lord Maugham wrote the notes which follow.

VI

NOTES BY LORD MAUGHAM

I. OBSERVATIONS IN RELATION TO THE
FACTS AND THE STATEMENTS IN THE
OVERBURY PAMPHLET

IT should be stated in the first place that there is no doubt whatever that the trials took place, though the only extant official records of the two trials which are set out verbatim on p. 78, are remarkably jejune.

The words 'posuit se culpabilem esse' are a little puzzling, since it is, I think, clear that John alone had admitted his guilt. It seems to me that the clerk may have used them as regards Joan and Richard to indicate that they were convicted on a confession by John that they as well as he were guilty, and perhaps he was unable to translate into Latin the phrase 'convicted on the admission of John that he [or she] was guilty'. Or again the entries against John and Richard may be due simply to error as to the actual facts.

The indictments in these cases have not survived, nor is there any record of the witnesses called for the Crown.

On the other hand, even apart from the entries above referred to, there is sufficient evidence that William Harrison's account of his disappearance from his house at Campden

on 16 August 1660 is a tissue of lies. His story as told by
Sir Thomas Overbury after his return to Campden some
two years later (the date is not stated) is full of the grossest
absurdities, most of which will be found stated in Mr.
Andrew Lang's account of the Campden Mystery and I
will only mention a few of them here.

He was seventy years of age and says he was attacked by
three mounted men with swords. It is clearly evident from
the tale that they wanted not only to rob him, but also to
kidnap him and sell him as a slave, which involved a sea
journey to North Africa or to Turkey or Smyrna. Harrison
had only 'a little cane' with which to defend himself, and
if capable of resisting at all should have fallen an easy prey;
but his story is that one of the men ran his sword into his
side and another wounded him from behind in the thigh.
This was strange behaviour for kidnappers who desired to
sell the old man in a distant land! 'They did not take my
money,' he says, 'but mounted me behind one of them,
drew my arms about his middle and fastened my wrists
together with something that had a spring-lock to it.' He
says nothing about being gagged. 'Later on they put a great
quantity of money into my pockets', and proceeded in the
same strange fashion across England to Deal which they
reached on the following Sunday, he being more dead than
alive all the time. He was then put on shipboard and his
wounds for the first time were dressed. I will not proceed
further to enumerate the absurdities of his story. The men
could not have taken him across England in this way without
being stopped and examined several times. An old man
with two body wounds would not be taken pillion across
England for a lawful reason. Moreover his value as a slave

would have been precisely nothing. Nor would any ship-master have incurred the risk of taking him on board without a substantial payment.

The tale of his return to Campden is almost equally strange. He says he was kept for a year and three-quarters by a physician eighty-seven years of age (name not given) who lived near Smyrna, at a town which is not named. This person had formerly been in England and knew Crowland in Lincolnshire, 'which he preferred before all other places in England'. When this master died, Harrison hastened to a port 'almost a day's journey distant'; but he does not name it. He got to Lisbon by a bribe of a silver bowl with which he had escaped and came across an Englishman (not named) who said he was 'born near Wisbeech in Lincolnshire'. (That town is in fact in Cambridgeshire.) He reached Dover and went to London where 'being furnished with necessaries', he 'came into the country'. No dates whatever are given of the return to England. He had a wife and a son at Campden, who presumably were the persons who would be rejoiced to hear of his marvellous escape and would furnish 'the necessaries'. There was a well-known road from London to Campden; but there is nothing in this 'true account' as to how he went from Dover to Campden and as to his reception in that place. At that time a poor man had to walk. Coaches were rare except on roads to important places and seats in them were expensive. An unknown old man in a dilapidated condition would not have procured a horse with saddle and bridle except by paying for them. Who advanced him the money for this journey through England?

If a man in a responsible position, aged seventy, leaves his home and his wife and family and disappears for two years, and then returns with a story which is completely untrue, I think we are justified in the conjecture that he is a rascal who disappeared for reasons of his own. Nor is this idea removed by the very calm spirit in which he refers in the 'true account' to the fate of the three Perrys. True it is that when Harrison left his home he could not have known that John Perry was likely to accuse himself and his relatives of murdering Harrison; but after all if Harrison had not left his home without a word to anyone, there would plainly have been no tragedy. In the disturbed state of England in 1660 any- one with any money on him who disappeared was very likely to have been murdered, and Harrison could not have failed to foresee the dark suspicions which might attach to his son and his servant. Those suspicions did in fact arise before John Perry had made any statement tending to incriminate himself or his mother or brother.

Moreover there are other grounds for suspicion in regard to Harrison. In particular I would refer to the finding by a poor woman in the highway between Ebrington and Camp- den, about half a mile from the latter, of the hatband and comb of Harrison, 'the hat and comb being hacked and cut and the band bloody' (Sir Thomas Overbury's account). I can see no reasonable explanation except that these articles were placed, or shall we say 'planted', in a spot where they were certain to be found on the following day in order to make people believe that Harrison had been murdered and thus to prevent any efforts to discover his whereabouts. Rejecting as we must the kidnapping story, and remembering that in Harrison's 'true and perfect account' he says he was wounded in the side and in the thigh, but does not account in any way for the hacked and cut hat and comb and the blood on the band, it seems to me much the most probable hypothesis that some person who was assisting Harrison in his disappearance had laid this false trail. It is unlikely to have been Harrison himself for the following reason. His recollection of the laying of the false trail seems to have faded away when he wrote his long letter to Sir Thomas Overbury, and it is not very likely that he would have forgotten all about it if he had himself placed the articles in the highway after having hacked and cut the hat and supplied the blood for the band. This was a very dramatic incident in his flight. But instead of mentioning the blows on his head, he invented two wounds on his body, a quite unnecessary and also a dangerous invention since if Overbury had asked for an explanation of this discrepancy and demanded to see the scars on the body Harrison's imposture might well have been disclosed. It seems to me probable that Harrison handed the hat, band, and comb to his helper with instruc-tions to place them in the highway and that the latter thought to improve on his orders by hacking the hat and adding some blood to the band, intending to make it clear that Harrison had been murderously attacked by sword blows on the head.

Who was the assistant? Once more it is only a matter for conjecture. I think it was probably John Perry. His account of his alleged wanderings when sent by Mrs. Harrison between eight and nine o'clock on the evening of 16 August to find his master seems to me to be strange and suspicious. When he got back to Harrison's house why did he lie in a hen-house instead of going to his own bed? And how could a resident at Campden lose his way on the highroad close to

his own home on setting out to go to Charringworth after
the moon had risen? The mist must have been a very un-
usual one if he could not keep between the hedges. Is not
the truth this, that Harrison had to be given time to get
away before a real search was made for him?

It is not unimportant to note that John Perry in one of his
various lying statements to Sir Thomas Overbury alleged
that after the (pretended) murder and his night in the hen-
house 'he carried the said hatband and comb and threw
them, after he had given them three or four cuts with his
knife, in the highway where they were after found'. Asked
for his reason for so doing he said 'he did it that it might be
believed his master had been there robbed and murdered'.
This may have been one of the few true statements in his
confused and contradictory allegations before Sir Thomas
Overbury.

John Perry was certainly a person subject to chronic
mental derangement (a paranoiac); and Sir Thomas Overbury, if he had been possessed of moderate intelligence,
should have discovered the fact very early in his interrogations. He seems to have been a very foolish person. I cannot
criticize his letter to Thomas Shirley in detail; but I may
refer the reader to a few things in it. First, the 'ball of inkle'
incident. Apart from the fact that a young man like Richard
would not have needed or used a woman's hair-lace to
strangle a man of seventy already overcome on the ground
(according to John Perry's confession), would Richard be
likely to retain the lethal instrument in his pocket for some
days after committing the murder? Secondly, the alleged
nose bleeding of Richard's two children when he met and
touched them on his way to church on the Sunday—

'which was looked upon as ominous'. Thirdly, the ridiculous story of the 'two men in white' in Campden garden not many weeks before Harrison's departure who attacked John Perry for no apparent reason, with naked swords. John, after defending himself with his sheep-pick, fled; but no one saw these men and it does not appear that they entered the house or took anything. Fourthly, the fact that the body of Harrison could not be found in any of the several places where John Perry said it was hidden. Fifthly, the fact that a search for the £140 which was stated to have been stolen from Harrison's house in the year preceding that of the alleged murder was unavailing. John had declared that with his connivance his brother Richard had stolen this money while the family were at church, and had buried it in the garden (which I take to mean Richard's garden), but no money could be found there. Lastly, a man of good sense would have hesitated a long time before believing the statement of such a person as John Perry that his own mother and brother had committed the crime. John was making it certain that he himself would be hanged. He might at least have left his mother out of it. An accusation of others, in a case where the accuser can get no benefit from it and where his own mother is an accused, is so rare that a magistrate worthy of the name would have required some real evidence beyond the confession of John before committing the mother and Richard for trial, in the face of their statements that they were completely innocent 'with many imprecations on themselves if they were in the least guilty'.

The question then remains, why did William Harrison abscond and return two years later with his fantastic story? That is the true Campden mystery. We are again left in the realm of conjecture: for we have not before us the factors which would justify any positive conclusion.[1] We know nothing about Harrison's relations with his wife and family, or, which may be equally important, with the Dowager Lady Campden. Nor do we know anything as to his pecuniary position. We are told, however, by the manuscript notes in Anthony Wood's copy of Overbury's pamphlet that his wife was believed to be 'a snotty covetuous presbyterian', and if this was so it may be assumed that the husband was of the same complexion.

Before hazarding a guess as to the truth it is important to remember the strange situation which had existed for over a year prior to 16 August 1660. Government by law in England had in effect ceased to exist on 7 May 1659 when Richard Cromwell ceased to act as protector and the five judges whom he had appointed no longer held office. The Long Parliament then purported to appoint certain judges, but the validity of their commissions was more than doubtful after that parliament was dissolved. There followed a period during which law had practically ceased to function. Till 8 May 1660 when Charles II was proclaimed, no one could be in any way confident that he would be restored to the throne; and it was not till 29 May when he entered London with the enthusiastic rejoicings of the people that the restoration became certain. In the meantime there were doubts, conspiracies, and risings of the military; but what

---

[1] Mr. H. R. Colman has noted as a coincidence an advertisement in *Mercurius Publicus* for 22 Aug. 1660, six days after Harrison's disappearance, calling for the apprehension of certain malefactors. Seven men, professing to search for Cornet Joyce, robbed a house at Grove, near Wantage, carried off the owner and his son to Bagley Wood, where they stole their horses and left them.

I think is not generally remembered is the position of the judges of the high court, of the justices of the peace, and indeed of all judicial officers. If there was to be a restoration of King Charles the judges must have perceived there would follow a recognition of the fact that they had never been legally appointed, and that all judgements, decisions, and acts would be held to be wholly illegal. Their lives as well as their estates were in danger. With the Cavaliers in power, those judges who had purported to sit in judgement in courts which lawfully could only derive their authority from the king, and who had delivered judgements of death or depriva/ tion of property, might well feel in the utmost jeopardy. Nor were the justices of the peace wholly free from danger.[1]

It should be added that the State was on the verge of bankruptcy and the pay of soldiers and sailors was in serious arrear—which was one of the difficulties attending the Restoration.

Historians have not, so far as I have been able to dis/ cover, dealt adequately with this aspect of the last months of the Interregnum, and with the practical cessation of the administration of justice which must have been a terrible feature of it, though some of them have used the ominous word 'anarchy'. The judges appointed since the death of Charles I were probably a little easier in their minds as re/ gards their acts as judges after the declaration of Breda became known throughout England. It was dated 14 April 1660 and promised among other things a general pardon;

[1] See as to the position of the judges, which was very confused, F. A. Inderwick, *The Interregnum* (1891); B. Whitelocke, *Memorials* (1853), iv. 461, 462; Siderfin's *Reports* and in particular the preface to the second part dealing with cases argued in 1657, 1658, and 1659.

but of course it did not validate any judicial acts, still less did it confer or promise to confer judicial powers on those persons who had been appointed to their offices under or during the Commonwealth. But one of the first measures undertaken by the Convention Parliament after the return of Charles was the Bill of Indemnity and Oblivion for all offences committed during 'the recent troubles'. It was under hot discussion between the two houses for three months and did not receive the royal assent until 29 August 1660. It may be noted here that William Harrison when he disappeared on 16 August obviously could not have been aware of the provisions of the Act.[1]

It seems to me at least probable that William Harrison's disappearance was in some way connected with the great change that took place in England on the restoration of the monarchy, and Mr. Andrew Lang's suggestion that he was 'a witness better out of the way' as knowing of some secret

---

[1] There were three Acts passed by parliament after the Restoration relating to the illegal judicial proceedings. The first was for the continuance of process and judicial proceedings commenced before 5 May 1660 in the name of Oliver, Lord Protector, or Richard, Lord Protector, though commenced or prosecuted in English. The second (cap. xi) was an Act of free and general pardon, indemnity, and oblivion. This was an elaborate Act of fifty-one sections. It provided, with exceptions for named regicides and some others, that all treasons, felonies, crimes, and misdemeanours since 1 Jan. 1637 and before 24 June 1660 should be 'pardoned, released, discharged and put in utter oblivion'. Section 10 contained exceptions for murder and certain other grave crimes. Section 44 is worth mention. It provided that those who since 5 December 1648 'gave sentence of death upon any person ... in any of the late illegal and tyrannical High Courts of Justice ... were made incapable of bearing any office ... or of serving as a member in any parliament after 5 Sept. 1660'. The third Act (cap. xii) confirmed generally but with important exceptions all judicial proceedings since 1 May 1642 by the illegal courts during the troubles.

connected with the troubled times, for instance the case of
one of the regicides, is certainly conceivable. It must, however, be observed that there does not appear to be the smallest
ground for thinking that Harrison was possessed of any
such secret. It could not I think have concerned the regicides,
for their actions (as the reports of their trials show) were by no
means secret. There appears to have been no mystery about
the Campden family. Juliana the dowager Lady Campden
had, it is said, employed Edward Harrison for nearly half a
century, and he was her steward in 1659 and 1660. Her
husband Edward Lord Noel died in 1642. She erected a
fine monument to his memory in 1664 and survived him
thirty-eight years. I cannot find that there was any difficulty
about the succession to the title or estates at this time.
Campden House was for the most part a ruin and the
dowager Lady Campden occupied a small portion of the
original mansion which was magnificent. Its destruction is
said to have been due to the fact that a predecessor of Edward
Lord Noel had set fire to it during the rebellion in order to
prevent it falling into the hands of the parliament troops. It
seems likely that Lady Campden was a loyalist, and this
makes it the less probable that Harrison was possessed of a
political secret such as Mr. Andrew Lang suggested.

We can do no more than guess at possibilities. A not too
unlikely possibility is that he had misapplied money belong-
ing to Lady Campden and that he absconded at the time
when he believed that his defalcations were about to be discovered. He knew that the Restoration would lead to the
appointment of king's judges and the holding of assizes at
Gloucester once more. The danger to which he was exposing others did not perhaps worry him. He returned when he

thought the Act of Indemnity would protect him, and when he had spent all the money he took with him. It seems most unlikely that a man like Harrison, with no means of obtaining references, and no capacity for doing hard manual work, could have earned money during his absence from Campden. When his money was spent he had to come home and to claim to be supported by his son who had succeeded to his father's position as steward to Lady Campden.

It is possible that the £140 in money alleged to have been stolen from Harrison, 'upon a market-day' some time in the year before his disappearance, was merely concealed and that it formed part of the funds with which he left on 16 August 1660. We may take it as certain that he took with him a good provision for his own support in a strange country.

I hesitate to believe that Mrs. Harrison was aware of her husband's intention to abscond or of his having carried out that intention. Such a hypothesis involves her in the terrible charge of having remained silent while three innocent persons were lying in jail for months and ultimately condemned to death for a supposed crime which had never been committed. William Harrison's reputation might of course have suffered if his wife had disclosed that he was probably alive; but it may be supposed that he was safely hidden under a false name. There were no police in those days. If, however, she did know the facts about her husband, one can well understand that the death of the three Perrys weighed terribly upon her mind, and caused her to commit suicide after her husband's return. (See the manuscript note to Anthony Wood's copy of Overbury's pamphlet.[1])

[1] Above, p. 32.

It should be added that there are a good many instances of persons with a remarkable form of mental disease accusing themselves and others of imaginary crimes. Some of these cases will be found in Paget's book.[1] The matter was also discussed in an address by Sir John Collie to the Medico-Legal Society on 16 June 1926 which is readily accessible in their records.

In concluding this note I wish to repeat that the matters touched upon are almost as uncertain as 'the songs the Sirens sang'; and I invite the curious reader before making up his mind as to the probable facts to peruse the two most interesting plays by Mr. John Masefield published in 1910 under the title of the *Tragedy of Nan and Other Plays*. These plays deal with facts taken from the Campden Tragedy, and they suggest possible circumstances which if accepted would serve to explain the Campden Mystery.

II. A NOTE IN RELATION TO
THE LAW INVOLVED IN THE CASE

It is a mistake to suppose, as some writers have suggested, that the case of the Perrys led to an alteration in the law. No less authorities than Sir Edward Coke and Sir Matthew Hale had already dealt with the matter. Coke in the third volume of his *Institutes* often cited as his 'Pleas of the Crown' refers in chapter 104 to a Warwickshire case which is worth citing both for its curious interest and his quaint conclusion.

'In the county of Warwick there were two brethren, the one having issue a daughter and being seized of lands in fee

[1] Above, pp. 36–55.

devised the government of his daughter and his lands, until she came to her age of sixteen years, to his brother, and died. The uncle brought up his niece very well both at her book and needle, etc. and she was about eight or nine years of age: her uncle for some offence correcting her, she was heard to say, "Oh good uncle kill me not." After which time the childe after much inquiry, could not be heard of, whereupon the uncle being suspected of the murder of her, the rather for that he was her next heir, was upon examination anno *8 Jac. regis* committed to the jail for suspicion of murder, and was admonished by the justices of assize to find out the childe, and thereupon bailed him until the next assizes. Against which time, for that he could not find her, and fearing what would fall out against him, took another childe as like unto her both in person and years as he could find, and apparelled her like unto the true childe, and brought her to the next assizes, but upon view and examination, she was found not to be the true childe; and upon these presumptions he was indicted and found guilty, had judgement and was hanged. But the truth of the case was, that the childe being beaten over night, the next morning when she should go to school, ran away into the next county, and being well educated was received and entertained of a stranger: and when she was sixteen years old, at what time she should come to her land, she came to demand it, and was directly proved to be the true childe.'

'Which case we have reported for a double caveat: first to Judges, that they, in case of life, judge not too hastily upon bare presumption; and, secondly, to the innocent and true man, that he never seek to excuse himself by false or undue means, lest thereby he offending God (the author of truth) overthrow himself, as the uncle did.' (Coke's *Institutes*, vol. iii. cap. 104.)

Sir Matthew Hale who died in 1676 dealt with the problem in his *History of the Pleas of the Crown* (vol. ii, p. 290) which, however, was not published till a later date.

'I would never convict any person of murder or manslaughter, unless the fact were proved to be done, or at least the body found dead for the sake of two cases, one mentioned in my Lord Coke's P.C. cap. 104, p. 232, a Warwickshire case. Another that happened in my remembrance in Staffordshire where *A* was long missing, and upon strong presumption *B* was supposed to have murdered him, and to have consumed him to ashes in an oven, that he should not be found, whereupon *B* was indicted of murder and convict and executed, and within one year after *A* returned, being indeed sent beyond sea by *B* against his will, and so though *B* justly deserved death, yet he was really not guilty of that offense for which he suffered.'

Hale (or his editor) says in a note that 'this was also a rule in the civil law Dig. Lib. xxix, Sit. 5, § 24'. And for those who like a Latin legal maxim I will add that after some observations on charges of witchcraft and rape, he concludes his chapter by observing, 'Potius semper est errare in acquietando quam in puniendo ex parte misericordiae, quam ex parte justiciae.' I am afraid that this maxim was not much regarded till long after the death of Hale.

The rule in cases of murder or manslaughter that either the body must be found or that there should be strong grounds for presuming the death is thus a very old one. It is founded on good sense, it is as Mr. Justice Maule stated 'a

rule of caution and prudence in cases of murder and man,
slaughter and not an absolute rule of evidence'.

In modern times the confession of John Perry would have
been admissible in evidence only against himself; and Mr.
John Paget and Mr. Andrew Lang both assume that that
was also the law in 1661. I think this was not so. It must
be remembered that at that time the rule of evidence exclud,
ing the admission of hearsay (from which the rule as to con,
fessions follows) had not been definitely laid down, and that
juries were entitled to return their verdicts upon private
knowledge or outside information.[1] In 1670 Sir Matthew
Hale laid it down, I think for the first time, that hearsay
from a witness was inadmissible as direct evidence, but even
he thought that hearsay might be allowed in corroboration
of direct evidence.[2] However, the general rule was not
finally laid down and certainly was not always observed
for many years after 1661. It may be mentioned that Scroggs
C. J. stated at the great trial of Green, Berry, and Hill for
murder that evidence as to a statement by Berry before
the Council was evidence against him only. In Lang,
horne's case he said in the course of Bedloe's evidence
that hearsay was not evidence. In my opinion Scroggs,
brutal as his behaviour was in many cases, was a good
lawyer.

It seems to be the fact that there was no settled rule in 1661
against the admission of hearsay evidence, and if so it must
in my view follow that it was probably not settled law at that
date that the confession of John could not be admitted
against his mother and brother. If the unsworn and untested

[1] R. V. Bushell, Vaughan, 135.
[2] Lutterell, Reynell, Mod. 282.

statement of *A* that he saw *B* and *C* committing a crime can be admitted as evidence against *B* and *C*, it would seem to be not the less admissible if *A* also accuses himself in the same statement. In most cases it would have more rather than less probative force.

But the law was changing at the relative time. In Kelyng's Reports (published after his death which occurred in 1671) it is stated that a confession is only evidence against the party who made it; but the passage appears to relate only to cases of high treason (see Kelyng's Reports, 2nd edn., p. 18, sect. 5). In Hawkins's *Pleas of the Crown*, vol. ii, p. 595, sect. 32 (I am quoting from the 8th edn.) I find the statement (not limited to treason cases) that it is 'agreed that the confession of one person cannot be given in evidence against others'. The margin, however, after a reference to St. Tr. 265 says: 'But see the contrary practised in Ellis's Case 1 St. Tr. 341; Throckmorton's Case 1 St. Tr. 63, 73; Duke of Norfolk's Case 1 St. Tr. 82; Earl of Essex's Case 1 St. Tr. 198; Sir Walter Raleigh's Case 1 St. Tr. 212.' This important work was, however, not published till 1716–21. It seems to me to show that in the early seventeenth century confessions were admitted against others than the parties who made them, and to leave the date of the change uncertain. The real criticism of the conduct of the trial by Sir Robert Hyde in 1661 is of a twofold character. On the one hand he does not seem to have had any idea of the necessity at least for great caution in a case where proof of death of the alleged victim was not forthcoming. On the other hand he apparently had no appreciation of the fact that John Perry's confession was that of a man with a deranged intellect even if not permanently insane. His statements, which I need not recapitulate, were both conflicting and in some respects absurd.

One thing, however, might be said in extenuation of Sir Robert Hyde's conduct, namely, that the three prisoners had pleaded guilty before Sir Christopher Turnor to the indict, ment for breaking into William Harrison's house in the year 1659 and robbing him of £140. This might lead to the conclusion that in any event they were malefactors. But he of course knew of the Act of Indemnity since they had ob, tained the benefit of it, and it was at least possible that they pleaded guilty to save trouble at the suggestion of lawyers or others in court who knew that either they were innocent or if guilty entitled to the benefit of the Act, and that the proceedings were sheer waste of time. In any case the question for Sir Robert Hyde was whether there was a case to go to the jury on the only indictment before him. The confession of John Perry was proved and it seems that evidence was also given about the 'ball of inkle' and of John's statement which amounted to a further confession by him. There might thus have been some evidence against John though it was quite insufficient in the remarkable circumstances of the case to justify a conviction in the absence of the body of Harrison; but no judge worthy of the name would have allowed the mother and brother to be convicted on the confession of such a man as John.

The truth appears to be that the judge was not worthy of the position. He seems to have been appointed a judge of the common pleas on 31 May 1660 (two days after Charles II entered London) by the influence of the earl of Clarendon who was his cousin. He was then sixty-five years old. By the same influence he was appointed chief justice of the king's bench on 19 October 1663; but he never acquired any reputation, and it may be that the story told in Anthony Wood's copy of Overbury's pamphlet (*supra*, p. 32) of his committing to prison the man who brought to Gloucester the news of Harrison's return, a quite illegal act, which afterwards must have caused him much trouble, is true. However, he died, presumably full of honours, 'en son study en Serjeant's Inn . . . le Vesper de mesme jour in que il fuit seant en le Court en le Matine' (Siderfin i, p. 253), and was buried in Salisbury Cathedral where he has a monument.

VII

MORE NEW EVIDENCE

In 1945 Mr. E. O. Winstedt of the Bodleian Library announced a discovery which made the mystery possibly less mysterious but certainly more fascinating than before.[1] Unsuspected by anyone there had been standing on the shelves of the Bodleian the two earliest accounts of it, at least one of which was published within a few months of William Harrison's alleged return. They are contained in a broadside-ballad and a pamphlet, both published in London by Charles Tyus. The pamphlet bears the date 1662, but the ballad is undated and so there is no means of knowing whether they came out simultaneously, or whether one of them came first and was such a success that the other followed. We begin with the ballad only because it is the shorter and livelier of the two. It belongs to Anthony Wood's collection.

Truth brought to Light: OR,

Wonderful strange and true news from Gloucester shire, concerning one Mr. William Harrison, formerly Stewart to the Lady Nowell of Cambden, who was supposed to be Murthered by the Widow Pery and two of her Sons, one of which was Servant to the

[1] In *Notes and Queries*, clxxxix (1945), 162.

said Gentleman. Therefore they were all three apprehended and sent to Gloucester Goal, and about two years since arraigned, found guilty, condemned, and Executed upon Broadway hill in sight of Cambden, the mother and one Son being then buried under the Gibbet, but he that was Mr. Harrisons Servant, hanged in Chains in the same place, where that which is remaining of him may be seen to this day, but at the time of their Execution, the said Mr. Harrison was not dead, but ere seven years were over should be heard of again, yet would not confess where he was, but now it appears the Widow Pery was a witch, and after her Sons had robd him, and cast him into a Stone Pit, she by her witch-craft conveyed him upon a Rock in the Sea near Turky, where he remained four days and nights, till a Turkish Ship coming by took him and sold him into Turky, where he remained for a season, but is now through the good providence of God returnd again safe to England, to the great wonder and admiration of all that know the same. This is undenyably true, as is sufficiently testified by Inhabitants of Cambden, and many others thereabouts.

To the Tune of, *Aim not too high.*[1]

Amongst those wonders which on earth are shown,
In any age there seldom hath been known,
A thing more strange then that which this Relation,
Doth here present unto your observation.

In *Glocestershire* as many know full well,
At *Cambden* Town a Gentleman did dwell,

[1] This tune was very popular especially for 'the metrical lamentations of extraordinary criminals'. Shakespeare knew it as the tune of 'Fortune my Foe' (*Merry Wives*, Act II, sc. 3). It is reproduced and its history is summarized in W. Chappell, *Popular Music of the Olden Times*, ed. H. E. Wooldridge (1893), i. 76–77.

Truth brought to Light

Slow

A - - mayst those won - ders which on earth are shown,

In a - ny age there sel - dom hath been known,

A thing more strange then that which this Re - lation,

Doth here pre - sent un - to your ob - ser - vation.

One Mr. *William Harrison* by name,
A Stewart to a Lady of great fame.

A Widdow likewise in the Town there was,
A wicked wretch who brought strange things to pass,
So wonderful that some will scarce receive,
These lines for truth nor yet my words believe.

But such as unto *Cambden* do resort,
They surely found this is no false report,
Though many lies are dayly now invented,
This is as true a Song as ere was Printed.

Therefore unto the story now give ear,
This Widow *Pery* as it doth appear,
And her two sons all fully were agreed,
Against their friend to work a wicked deed.

One of her sons even from a youth did dwell,
With Mr. *Harrison* who loved him well,
And bred him up his Mother being poor,
But see how he requited him therefore.

For taking notice that his Master went,
Abroad to gather in his Ladies rent,
And by that means it was an usual thing,
For him great store of money home to bring.

He thereupon with his mischevous mother,
And likewise with his vile ungodly Brother,
Contriv'd to rob his Master, for these base
And cruel wretches were past shame and grace.

One night they met him comming into Town,
And in a barbarous manner knockt him down,
Then taking all his money quite away,
His body out of sight they did convey.

But being all suspected for this deed,
They apprehended were and sent with speed,
To *Glocester* Goal and there upon their Tryal,
Were guilty found for all their stiff denyal.

The second part to the same Tune.

It was supposed the Gentleman was dead,
And by these wretches robd and Murthered,
Therefore they were all three condem'd to death,
And eke on *Broadway-hill* they lost their breath.

One of the Sons was buried with his Mother,
Under the Gibbet, but the other Brother,
That serv'd the Gentleman was hang'd in Chains,
And there some part of him as yet remains.

But yet before they died they did proclaim
Even in the ears of those that thither came,
That Mr. *Harison* yet living was
And would be found in less then seven years space.

Which words of theirs for truth do now appear
For tis but two year since they hanged were,
And now the Gentleman alive is found
Which news is publisht through the Countrys round.

But lest that any of this truth shall doubt,
Ile tell you how the business came about.
This Widow *Pery* as tis plainly shown
Was then a Witch although it was not known.

So when these Villains by their mothers aid
Had knockt him down (even as before was said)
They took away his money every whit,
And then his body cast into a pit.

He scarce was come unto himself before
Another wonder did amaze him more,
That whilst he lookt about, he found that he
Was suddainly conveyed unto the Sea.

First on the shore he stood a little space
And thence unto a rock transported was,
Where he four days and nights did then remain
And never thought to see his friends again.

But as a Turkish ship was passing by
Some of the men the Gentleman did spy,
And took him and as I understand,
They carried him into the Turkish Land.

And there (not knowing of his sad disaster),
They quickly did provide for him a Master,
A Surgeon or of some such like profession,
Whose service he performed with much discretion.

It seems in gathering Hearbs he had good skill,
And could the same exceeding well distil,
Which to his Master great content did give,
And pleas'd him well so long as he did live.

But he soon dyd, and at his death he gave him,
A piece of plate that so none should enslave him,
But that his liberty he might obtain,
To come into his native land again.

And thus this Gentleman his freedom bought,
And by a *Turky* Ship from thence was brought,
To *Portugal*, and now both safe and sound,
He is at length arrived on English ground.

Let not this seem incredible to any,
Because it is an end afirmed by many,
This is no feigned story, though tis new,
But as tis very strange tis very true.

You see how far a Witches power extends,
When as to wickedness her mind she bends,
Great is her Malice, yet can God restrain her,
And at his pleasure let her loose or chain her.

If God had let her work her utmost spight,
No doubt she would have kild the man outright,
But he is saved and she for all her malice,
Was very justly hang'd upon the Gallows.

Then let all praise to God alone be given,
By men on earth as by the Saints in heaven,
He by his mercy dayly doth befriend us,
And by his power he will still defend us.

London. Printed for Charles Tyus at the
three Bibles on London-Bridge.

THE
POWER OF WITCHCRAFT
BEING

A most strange but true Relati-
on of the most miraculous and won-
derful deliverance of one Mr. William
Harrison, of Cambden, in the Coun-
ty of Glocester, Steward to the Lady
Nowell

Who was supposed to have been murthered by his own Servant,
and his Servants Mother and Brother: But to the amazement of all
people that live near the said place, the truth is now brought to
light; and Mr. Harrison after above two years absence is returned
into his own Country and place of abode in Cambden.

The manner how he was bewitched away, and the manner of his
safe return back again into his own Countrey you shall hear in this
following Discourse.

London printed for Charles Tyus at the three Bibles
on London-bridge, 1662.

That the Lord hath been pleased wonderfully to shew forth his power to sinful man, it doth every day appear unto us; there is not a month nor week, nay we may say a day in the year in which the mighty works of the Lord are not visibly apparent unto us. But that which I have now to relate unto you is most wonderful, nay I may say a most amazing providence as ever man or woman ever heard in this Kingdom, it may be truly said to be a discovery of Witchcraft; and that the Lord doth sometimes suffer wicked people to have power over others in bewitching them the Scriptures hold forth, for we read of *Saul* that he went to the *Witch of Ender*, 1 *Sam. 28. vers. 6.* And in several places of Scripture it doth evidently make clear unto us, That the Lord hath suffered Witches and Sorcerers, and such like people in a Nation.

But I shall not stand to give you any examples of old; but come to the matter intended which is as follows.

It was not much above two years since there dwelt at *Cambden* in *Glocestershire* one Master *William Harrison*, a Gentleman of good credit and estimation in the place where he dwelt. This Master *Harrison* aforesaid was Steward to the honourable Lady the Lady *Nowel* whose place of dwelling was at *Cambden* also. In this place there was also a widow woman whose name was *Perry*, who had two sons; Master *Harrison* looking upon the woman as an honest poor woman, took one of her Sons from her, and brought him up at length to become one of his Houshold Servants. This Boy being grown up to be a lusty Fellow, observing his Master oftentimes to bring home great sums of money which he received for rent, being Steward to the Lady aforesaid: what doth this wicked fellow do but presently fell to contrive how he might become Master of some of those sums of money which he observed his Master so often to bring home.

It was not long but this fellow with his mother (who as it now appears was a Witch) with his other Brother did determine to set upon this Gentleman, as he should come along upon the road to his habitation to take what money he had from him, and there was an opportunity fell out so that they had an occasion to put their wicked determinations into practice, as you shall hear; The Gentleman was coming home, and being not many miles from his intended journeys end, this Widow *Perry* and her two sons met Mr. *Harrison*, who they no sooner espied, but they knockt him down and robbed him, and cast him into a pit whereout they digged stones. He did not long remain there, as you will hear by the sequel. But Mr. *Harrison* not coming home according to his usual custom, his Wife and Family were much troubled at it: Great search after some few days were made for him, but all to little purpose, for there was no tidings of him, but every one concluded that he was murthered upon the rode. It was not long before the Lord had brought to light this strange accident; for this widow *Perry* and her two Sons were suspected of the robbery, and they were all three forthwith apprehended, and at the Assizes at *Glocester* about two years hence, they were arraigned, condemned and executed for the supposed murther of Master *Harrison*.

The place of their execution was on *Broadway* hills in the sight of *Cambden* where a Gibbet was erected, the mother and one of her Sons were hanged and buried under the Gibbet, the other Son, who was Servant to Mr. *Harrison* was hanged in chains on the Gibbet, where part of him remains to be seen at this day.

At the time of their Execution they would not confess what they had done with Master *Harrison*; but said that he was not dead, but ere seven years were half over they should see Master *Harrison* again.

Now attend to this following Discourse, and you shall hear in what a condition Master *Harrison* was left in. This Widow *Perry* by her wicked Conjuration had power on Master *Harrison*, for no sooner had they knocked him down, and taken what he had from him, but they threw him into a pit; He had not lain long but he began to come to himself, and he apprehended where he was, but before he was come to himself fully, he was in a moment conveyed to the Sea Side, and from thence in a very short time he was conveyed to a rock standing in the Sea on the coast of Turky, where he remained the space of four days bare headed, his hat being left near *Cambden*, where they first had knocked him down.

After his four days abode there, there came by a Turkish ship which took him in, and brought him to Turky, and there sold him. His Master that bought him was by profes- sion a Chyrurgeon, who asked his new bought Servant what he could do, he answered his Master that then was, that he had skill in Gardening and could distil Hearbs, in which employment he was entertained in; and he so well behaved himself that he gained a great deal of love from his Master during his life.

He had not lived there above two years or thereabouts, but it pleased God his Master dyed, who out of the respect he did bear to Master *Harrison*, his Servant, he gave him a peice of plate, and bade him make use thereof for his Transportation into his own Country, which he did. After this it was not long but he heard of a Turky Merchant bound for *Portugal*, for the which piece of plate he had his passage to *Portugal*, where it was not long but he safely arrived, and is now since that come safely into his own Native Country, *England*, and is come to his own dwelling house at *Cambden*, to the no little astonishment and wonderful amazement of all his Friends and Relations, nay of all the Country round.

It is a matter of great amazement to all people that such a thing should be wrought by Witchcraft; but the truth of this is not to be disputed, for there are thousands of people that can witness and testifie the truth hereof.

Now friends; having related to you the truth of the whole matter, here is great matter of wonder and astonishment to all people, to see the wonderful deliverance which the Lord hath bestowed upon this Gentleman, and no question but he will and doth acknowledge the Lords mercy to him; We may also observe here how the Lord doth[1] bring punishment upon such wicked livers as this Woman and her two Sons were, you may look but into the *22. of Exod. 18* where it is said, *thou shalt no suffer a witch to live*, and here we may see how just the Lord was in his dealing to these vile and wicked livers, for soon after they had committed the wicked fact on such a faithful friend as this Mr. *Harrison* was, who out of love and pity did bring up this Boy and kept him as we may say as his own, the Lord was pleased to bring them to this sad end and deserved punishment, and I wish that it may prove a warning to all others that practice such divelish and horrid Witchcrafts.

In the 5. of *Micah* and the 12. *verse*, the Lord hath promised

[1] In the original: both.

there, that he will cut off Witchcrafts, and there shall be no more Soothsayers, the Lord will not be worse than his word, but he will bring all such wicked offenders to shame/ful ends, he will not only punish them here, but hereafter, for Witches and Wizards or fortunetellers and the like, they are such as sell their souls to the Devil to do mischief, and though the Lord let them alone for a season to go on in their wicked ways, yet let them know that there will be a reckon/ing day come, when they shall pay dearly for all their folly.

O that this notable example of Gods Justice, might be a warning peice unto all of us, of what condition soever we be, and this wonderful example of mercy to Mr. *Harrison* might be always fresh in our memory. Surely we may judge the Lord dealt by him as he did by *Job*, when the Lord gave Satan leave to do what he would with him, *onely touch not his life* (saith God) as we may read in the first Chapter of the Book of *Job*. So the Lord would not suffer this wicked woman to do any hurt to his person, that is, to his life, as we now may see: Although every one thought that he had been murthered, the Lord can and the Lord will restrain the power of the wicked, they shall not always have their will, though he doth give them power, yet doth put a restraint upon them; and they cannot go any further then he will give them leave.

What matter of encouragement is here to all that love the Lord, the Lord may and doth suffer Satan the great Enemy of mankind to tempt his people, and he doth sometimes let the wicked prevail, so far as to have some power of them, that is to do some mischief either to their bodies or estates and the like, but they cannot hurt their soul for the Lord taketh care of that, and he will preserve them, in spite of all the Devils in Hell.

I shall now come to a conclusion; only I shall desire every one that hears this truth, to consider of the power of the Lord, and of the great mercy the Lord hath to bestow on them that desire sincerely to serve him, and I shall desire all that hear of this to consider of it, and to be careful of their ways, and to be watchful, for your adversary the Devil walketh about like a roaring Lyon, seeking whom he may devour, a Christian had need to be wakeful in sinful times, for it may be the occasion of any of us, to be often abroad, we had need to be careful of our selves, especially our souls, for that may fall out in a moment to us, which we nor any of our Relations little thought of.

The Devil is a very busy adversary, and is always contriving and plotting to do mischief to Gods people, where he can set any at work, he will promise great rewards to them, we read in the Scripture that he tempted our Lord Jesus Christ himself, *all this will I give thee*, saith he, *if thou wilt fall down and worship me*, but he could make no approach upon Christ, but upon poor sinful man, he doth too too often prevail, he strives all he can to make a Christian forsake the ways of God, it is Satans chief design and aim to tempt a Christian to make him think evil of the ways of God, that so at length he may bring them to himself, and this thou mayest assure thy self of, that if thou make a contract with the Devil, as all such wicked creatures do, as go by the name of Witches or Conjurers and the like, though thou dost reign in thy wicked ways for many months or years, yet know for certain that the Devil that set thee on work will pay thee thy wages.

I therefore now make an end, I wish that this Example of Mercy and Justice may be a seasonable warningpiece to us all, and that it may make every one that hears of it extoll the goodness of the Lord in so miraculously preserving the life of this Gentleman: And on the other side we have great cause to admire at this strange Providence, that the Lord would bring such wicked offenders to such a deserved punishment.

The Lord grant that we may live always to the praise of his holy Name while we live in the world, that when our time is finished in this life, we may inherit the Crown of Glory in the life which is to come.

FINIS.

There is nothing on the face of them to distinguish the ballad and the pamphlet, as to their veracity, from the innumerable stories of witchcraft, crime, and marvels which were printed in those days for the benefit of credulous readers. We know at most only one small fact about the impression they made at the time. Among the collections of the acquisitive Anthony Wood preserved in the Bodleian Library is a little almanac for the year 1662 in which he wrote notes opposite some of the dates. Opposite 6 August he wrote: 'Mr. Harrison of . . . supposed to be murthered 2 years ago, came out of Turkie to his home in the country.' Later, in different ink, he added: 'I have the pamphlet.' Even from these entries it cannot be inferred with certainty that Wood had seen the Tyus pamphlet. Unlike that of the ballad, the Bodleian copy was not originally among his papers. The second entry, being later, may refer not to this pamphlet at all, but to Overbury's *True and Perfect Account*; but neither of these authorities gives the date 6 August. It therefore seems most likely that Wood's first entry reproduces something that he had heard by word of mouth.

If Wood heard the supernatural part of the story he did not trouble to mention it; but although it must have appeared ridiculous even to some of those who sang the ballad, we cannot dismiss the writer or writers as indifferent to truth. The agreement between the story in verse and the story in prose is remarkably close. In prose it is longer, but the additions consist of edifying reflections, not of fictitious details. Either one of the two versions follows the other or both follow their authority faithfully.

We are thus presented with a new problem, the classical problem of *Quellenforschung* or the investigation of sources. We have before us three documents, giving two conflicting accounts of the same events; we must see how they are related to one another, and try to explain the discrepancies. Our first impulse will be to say that the earlier story is patently fabulous, and that the second, though far from convincing, largely eliminates the element of witchcraft and must have been substituted for it. If, for instance, Sir Thomas Overbury had seen the earlier story and disbelieved it, he may have made it plain to William Harrison that he would have to give a better account of his experiences in his signed statement. Looking closely we find, however, that in one respect the earlier account, though it gives less detail, runs better than the later. Harrison says that he claimed to have some skill in physic and so was bought by a grave physician, who employed him to keep his distilling-room, but on one occasion set him to gather cotton-wool. The Tyus pamphlet says that a surgeon, after buying Harrison, asked him what he could do, was told that he had skill in gardening and could distil herbs and set him to this employment. Probably Harrison knew of the earlier story and for some reason modified it in the later. The earlier story may be somebody's version of something Harrison himself had said. A scholar familiar with the popular writings of the period may discover that there already existed in some chapbook or pamphlet a tale of a Christian slave whose master was a physician and gave him a silver bowl. The ballad-monger and the pamphleteer may have rummaged out some such padding to fill in the blank in the biography of Harrison, or they may have received it along with the story of the disappearance and the trials. There are several possibilities, and we are not in a position to do more than guess which is the truth.

The reader may guess for himself. His guess may depend partly on his views about the belief in witchcraft. In the earlier stages of our investigation we saw that this superstition, though it did not cause the main miscarriage of justice, brooded over Campden at that time: Joan Perry was reputed a witch, at least by the time of the hangings, and Sir Matthew Hale believed in sorcery. Now we find that it was as a seasonable warningpiece against witchcraft that the story was first published. Perhaps as a result of the bloodshed and confusion of the preceding years, perhaps as a result of the aberrations of religious beliefs, there was a marked increase at this very time in the numbers of trials and executions of witches in England. But simultaneously here, as throughout western Europe, common sense and humanity resisted this cruel prejudice, and by the time when Overbury's pamphlet was published the tide was turning. We know that he was against persecuting dissenters and papists; he may also have been sceptical about witchcraft. However poorly we may think of him as a detective, he deserves credit for banishing this ingredient from his narrative.

One modern writer, Mr. Hugh Ross Williamson, has indeed constructed an explanation of the whole series of events in which witchcraft plays a far greater part than in the contemporary writings. It is given in a novel called *The Silver Bowl*, published in 1948. There is no need to discuss it here, or to show how many unfounded assumptions are worked into it, because in a later work, with a professedly historical purpose, the same writer drops the supernatural explanation.[1] He adds in this essay some information supplied by the Hon. Mrs. E. M. Bellingham. This consists of some data about underground passages and the statement that among the Campden papers there is a letter sent by hand from Algiers, from the third Viscount Campden to his mother 'Lady Juliana' asking for money from the estate, as well as a receipt and an accompanying letter for money received 'by hand of Harrison, oure good servant, who returneth forthwithe, and as I will later'.[2]

As it is not stated when these letters were written, nor whether that which refers to Harrison came from Algiers, which is more than 1,500 miles from Smyrna, it is impossible to make any use of them here. The Campden papers may indeed yet throw some light on the mystery.

[1] In *Historical Whodunits* (1957). For the benefit of foreign readers it should be explained that 'whodunit', who done it, is a colloquial term meaning a detective story. The theory set out in *The Silver Bowl* is summarized by K. Hickson in *Chambers's Journal*, Dec. 1953.

[2] pp. 177–9.

Even if there is no mention of it in surviving family corre-
spondence, there may be estate-records, leases, and accounts
and so forth, from which the dates of John and Edward
Harrison's employment as stewards may be settled. Unfortunately the present owner of the estate does not, as far
as he knows, possess any such papers from this period.
Attempts to hunt out anything of the kind among the
archives of the earl of Gainsborough, the heir of the vis-
counts Campden, at Exton in Rutland, have been unsuccessful. But another happy discovery has gone most of the way
to remedying this deficiency, and has added something
further.

This discovery was due not to good luck but to good
management and apposite knowledge. England's wealth of
private historical records is like its mineral wealth before the
industrial revolution, incompletely explored, apparently in-
exhaustible, rich beyond calculation. Until a few years ago
most of the little band of historians and antiquaries were
satisfied to dig what they needed from the open seams of the
great public repositories, with an occasional excursion, pick
in hand, to some private country muniment room. Times
are changing; country houses are vacated; records go adrift;
and historians are less easily satisfied. So far the mechaniza-
tion of research has not seriously begun, but with microfilms
and collating machines, and electronic catalogues we are
beginning an exploitation of our historical materials which
may go as far in the next century as the devouring of our
coal-measures has gone in this. One sign of the times is the
rise of county record-offices, and Gloucester is one of the
county towns which provide this admirable service. Mr.
Irvine Gray, the records officer at the Shire Hall, has ex-

tended his inquiries to records of all kinds all over the county, and a few years ago he followed up the fact that Chipping Campden had an ancient grammar school. It proved that the governors of the school have valuable archives. Among them is a volume of accounts which gives precious details of the work of their predecessors, the feoffees, in the seventeenth century. It shows a body such as might be found in a country town today. The neighbouring mag-nates sit down to do their business along with respectable, but much humbler, townsmen. The political and social education of the English people could hardly be more vividly illustrated than by their signatures appended when they approved the school accounts. There was Endymion Porter of Aston-sub-Edge, traveller, courtier, and friend of poets. There were feoffees who could not write their names but signed with a mark.

When this volume came into the hands of Mr. A. T. Gaydon, the assistant archivist, he immediately saw the significance of the names of two of the feoffees, and he has most generously allowed us to publish what he saw. Sir Thomas Overbury and William Harrison were both there. The feoffees used to meet twice a year to pass the accounts, once in the spring and once in the autumn. Harrison attended both meetings in 1657. At the spring meeting of 1658 Overbury was there too, so they had met before Harrison's disappearance. The disappearance leaves its traces: Harrison missed the six meetings after 5 April 1660 and before 15 October 1663. Overbury, as it happened, was at the first of these meetings, but he also missed the next four and he did not meet Harrison again at the board until 15 October 1663. Are we to infer that Harrison did not

SIGNATURES OF WILLIAM HARRISON
from the Chipping Campden Grammar School Account Book
(slightly enlarged)
The dates, in order, are 9 April 1657, 5 April 1660, 15 October 1663.

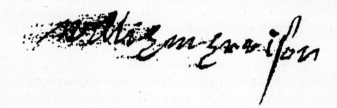

HARRISON'S SIGNATURES

The dates, in order, are 28 April 1664, 18 October 1664, 16 April 1672.

The horizontal line in the last signature need not be anything but a customary sign of abbreviation.

fully resume his place in local affairs until more than a year after his return, and that he did not come to a grammar school meeting until Overbury could be there to keep him in countenance? The facts are compatible with this conjecture, but they do not prove it.

After this Harrison put in twelve more appearances, the last of them on 16 April 1672. He was absent only three times, and it seems probable that, as he was then about eighty, he must have died not long after. Different people at different times have tried to find the dates of his birth and death, or those of his wife, in local records, but unsuccessfully, and these dates could scarcely help to elucidate his mystery. In case any reader may be able to coax yet more from the grammar school signatures we append a list of the dates on which Harrison and Overbury signed the accounts. We also give photographic facsimiles of Harrison's signatures. There are graphologists who claim that they can tell from such evidence how a man's character altered or what was his state of mind when he wrote. It would be interesting to have the judgement of such an expert, provided he did not know the story.

Dates on which Chipping Campden Grammar School accounts are signed by William Harrison and Thomas Overbury as feoffees.

9 Apr.	1657	Harrison	
16 Oct.	,,	Harrison	
15 Apr.	1658	Harrison	Overbury
12 Oct.	,,	neither	
12 Apr.	1659	neither	
6 Oct.	,,	neither	

5 Apr. 1660	Harrison	
11 Oct. „	—	Overbury
28 Mar. 1661	neither	
15 Oct. „	neither	
3 Apr. 1662	neither	
14 Oct. „	neither	
10 Apr. 1663	—	Overbury
15 Oct. „	Harrison	Overbury
28 Apr. 1664	Harrison	Overbury
18 Oct. „	Harrison	Overbury
31 Mar. 1665	—	Overbury
24 Oct. „	Harrison	
13 Apr. 1666	Harrison	Overbury
18 Oct. „	Harrison	
2 Apr. 1667	Harrison	Overbury
17 Oct. „	Harrison	
26 Mar. 1668	neither	
20 Oct. „	—	Overbury
22 Apr. 1669	neither	
28 Sept. „	Harrison	
21 Apr. 1670	Harrison	
11 Oct. „	—	Overbury
28 Mar. 1671	Harrison	
3 Oct. „	Harrison	
16 Apr. 1672	Harrison	

Overbury signs regularly from 4 Oct. 1675 until 12 Apr. 1683.

Others besides historians and lawyers have written about this mystery. We have mentioned a novel.[1] In late Victorian

---

[1] Hugh Ross Williamson, *The Silver Bowl* (1948).

days there was an actor, 'old Tom Holloway' who used to tour the western counties, playing melodrama and knock-about farce in tents and halls, with seats at 1s. and 3d. His repertory included an old play on this subject, said to be of 1830.[1] If it exists in print it will be worth reading as a curiosity and something more, however crude it may be; but, if it follows the real story at all closely, it will lack two essentials of the traditional melodrama, a heroine and a final triumph of justice. Another dramatist of a very different order who knew of this play but had never seen it was Mr. John Masefield. Lord Maugham has written on an earlier page that Mr. Masefield's two plays, *The Campden Wonder* and *Mrs Harrison*, suggest possible circumstances which would serve to explain the mystery, that is to say the remaining mystery of William Harrison's unknown adventures. The suggestions, to put them shortly, are that Harrison was paid £300 by Lord Campden to disappear; that he was never more than twenty miles away; that the drunken and ruffianly John Perry was in the secret. After a quarrel with his self-righteous brother Richard, in which their mother sides with Richard, John destroys them all by the false confession, and Harrison, though he knows of the trials, does not reveal himself, even to his wife, until his accomplice is out of the way. If this were all true, it would indeed explain a great deal, but it rests on at least five assumptions which are entirely unsupported by evidence. It still leaves two questions open: What advantage could arise from Harrison's

[1] For references to this or other companies touring with the play early in the present century, see Sir Barry Jackson, 'Barnstorming Days' in *Studies in English Theatre History* (Society for Theatre Research, 1952); *Theatre Notebook*, iii. 43 and iv. 3; and J. Linton in *The World's Fair*, 7 March 1959, p. 29.

disappearance for Lord Campden or any other third party? and, What change in the situation made it safe for him to reappear?

We need not pursue this line of thought. Mr. Masefield does indeed work up the details of the Overbury text with keen and attentive precision. He alters the timing for dramatic effect, for instance by making Harrison walk in a few minutes after the executions; but this poetic licence helps him to bring the story to life so that even when we only read his plays, without seeing them acted, we seem to see and hear and know the characters. This was what Mr. Masefield intended: his interest was in the Harrisons and the Perrys, in what they did to one another and what they suffered, not in the mysteriousness of the story. He gives us the shock of William Harrison's unannounced return; but he does not build up any suspense beforehand about whether Harrison is not dead after all; he does not start us on detec‑ tive guesses. The two main impressions that he enforces are the deadly antagonism between the brothers and the tragedy of 'poor folk wrong accused'. Their unending tragedy is one of the human realities which he has brought home in others of his works, not least in another Gloucestershire play about crime and punishment. This was published together with these two, and it is the greater work, on the stage almost unbearably poignant, called *The Tragedy of Nan*.

This tragic poet used the same materials as the historians, but where the materials were vague and ambiguous he had to be concrete and decided. We have more or less reliable reports of a few remarks actually made by the characters, but he had to tell the whole story in words put into their mouths. He used his art to make them living individuals, and to bring them close to the reader: except for the hard-hearted parson all the characters seem more familiar because they speak in dialect. One of the two plays was acted in a London theatre, and with the production this filling-out of the facts was carried farther. Less room was left for the spectator than for the reader to picture the figures or hear their speeches according to his own fancy. The six charac-ters were now four real men and two real women each with a real face and build, with postures and gestures, and a voice, imposing an interpretation on the written words. The part of John Perry was acted by Norman McKinnel, and anyone who remembers him in other parts will know how his brutal rage and sullen obstinacy must have domi-nated the scene.

Were these artists, the writer and the actors, doing essentially the same thing as the historians and the other scholars, though in their own, different way? Were they not reconstructing an historical incident, as it is sometimes claimed that historians do? Their version of it was tragic, evoking pity and terror; but there are also historians who occupy themselves with life in its tragic aspect, and this activity is no less proper to history than the legal study of a trial or the eliciting of the actual events from a muddle of lies and misunderstandings. A novelist or a dramatist can achieve a kind of authenticity by connecting his creative imagination with something that really happened, and it may seem too severe a rule for the historian that he must not improvise when information fails him, or force a conclusion when he is in doubt. In any case there will always be roman-tic historians and historical romances, and it will never be easy to draw a line between them. But there will also always be a hard and fast distinction between historians who do their best to conform to truth and those who eke it out with more pliable metal. One of the great English poets, who did as much as any of our professed historians to deepen and vivify our knowledge of the past, thought much about these problems. In his old age he asked the question again and gave his final answer:

> Friend, did you need an optic glass,
>   Which were your choice? A lens to drape
> In ruby, emerald, chrysopras,
>   Each object—or reveal its shape
> Clear outlined, past escape,
>   The naked very thing?

Browning's answer was that he had heard a Voice 'which straight unlinked fancy from fact'.

Hitherto we have been following the process by which truth has been gradually brought to light, and we have seen that criticism and discoveries of new facts have yielded some definitive results. The process has not been advanced by the roving imaginations which have also played around it. Many fancies have emerged, only to be discarded in the end. None of them seems to have suggested any hypothesis which has subsequently been confirmed. That may indeed happen in the course of historical research; all that we can say is that in this particular investigation it has not been so. It may yet be so in the future. Someone may spin a new network of explanations unsupported by evidence, which may be proved true by a fresh discovery of facts, or may remain unproved but too plausible to be rejected. In the meantime, even if nothing more emerges from the application of the established methods of research, there is another direction in which we may advance, the summoning of new techniques to the criticism of the materials that we already possess.

We have mentioned graphology as such a new technique. It may not have any notable successes to its credit in historical research. Its positive value is still trifling in comparison with that of photographic and other methods of science applied to the study of manuscripts, but it does attempt, and claim, to be genuinely scientific, and its textbooks are to be seen on the referenceshelves of some of the great manuscript collections. Without exaggerating its importance we may at least say that it has made some progress, and largely because it has been invigorated by the influence of modern psychology. To the layman it appears to be a branch of applied psychology, and to exemplify one of the main characteristics of contemporary psychology, that of drawing considerable inferences from small indications from which uninstructed common sense learns nothing at all. Coming back to our main subject we may remark that none of our authorities so far has made any use of the kind of psychology which is popularly supposed to have begun with Freud. Lord Maugham hoped for further enlightenment from a study by a psychologist, and this has fortunately been provided by Dr. Russell Davis, who is Reader in Psychopathology in the University of Cambridge. With this expert witness, who gives his opinion on the present state of our knowledge of the case, we conclude our volume.

VIII

SOME POINTS OF
PSYCHOLOGICAL INTEREST

By D. RUSSELL DAVIS

I

To start with a commonplace example—an acquaintance recently returned from a holiday abroad remarks that in a certain place the hotels are dirty and expensive. This information may be put to two uses. We may incorporate it either into what we already know of the place or into what we already know of the informant.

If we are interested in the place, perhaps because we are planning to take a holiday there, we piece together a picture of the conditions from what we are told by informants who have been there. We do not expect their accounts to be fully concordant with one another. We give weight to one account because it is consistent and we believe the informant to be a reliable observer. We discount what another informant tells us because it is inconsistent, or because it is not confirmed. Although we thus make judgements on each of the accounts given us, and perhaps also on the informants, our purpose is to arrive at the facts about the place.

Historians and lawyers proceed likewise. They make use of the information available to them in order to build up a picture of the conditions and events in a certain place at a certain time. Thus they have examined the available evidence in order to answer the question: What happened at Chipping Campden in the night of Thursday, 16 August 1660? In doing so they have taken note of the demeanour of the various witnesses and the degree of consistency in the statements attributed to them. In particular, they have tended to discount John Perry's statements as evidence, because they are neither plausible nor consistent, and because they are in conflict with other information. Discredited as a witness, he has been regarded as a rogue and a liar, a fool or insane. Although to a psychologist the judgements on his statements might appear reasonable, the diagnoses, on the other hand, would appear crude and inexpert.

Let us return to the remark about the hotels. It also tells us something about our acquaintance. For instance, that he speaks of the hotels and not the youth hostels or the boarding houses tells us broadly what kind of person he is in one respect. Also, his reference to dirt and expense may perhaps confirm a suspicion that he belongs to that class of obsessional person who shows an undue concern about such matters. Our point of view is now that adopted by psychologists, when they make use of the remarks made by a patient in order to build up a picture of his interests and attitudes. Thus a psychologist might examine the statements attributed to John Perry in order to answer the question: What kind of person was he?

In giving an answer to this type of question, a psychologist sometimes relies on the evidence of the patient's statements alone. He does not inspect the places about which a patient complains, for instance, or seek other information about them, before concluding that his concern about cleanliness is a symptom of an obsessional neurosis, when the manner and the terms in which he expresses his complaints are distinctive. Thus he may make this diagnosis if the patient is preoccupied and disturbed by thoughts about dirt, or some other matter, and if the patient recognizes himself that he is so to an immoderate or irrational degree. On the other hand, he may conclude that the complaints about dirt are delusional, and that the patient suffers from a psychosis, if he shows no awareness that they are extravagant and expresses them in vague and incoherent terms.

Similarly we might try to make a diagnosis in the case of John Perry without knowing what happened to William Harrison in the night of 16 August. But we should be greatly handicapped by other shortcomings in the evidence. For one thing, the significance to be given to statements depends upon the setting in which they are made. Suppose that our acquaintance's remark was made in answer to the question 'How did you like Florence?' and that he replies: 'The hotels there were dirty and expensive. I decided to move on immediately. Dirt always upsets me.' Now suppose that he replies: 'I was enthralled. The hotels there were dirty and expensive, but I would put up with any discomfort to see such paintings.' We might well conclude in the first instance that he is over-concerned about dirt; we would be less inclined to do so in the second instance, even if we have reason to believe his opinion about the hotels to be wrong. We may make tentative judgements about the informant in these instances, but our ignorance of the setting in which John Perry made his accusations against himself and his mother and brother is serious and is one reason for caution in making a diagnosis.

There is another, more interesting reason for caution. What we do know of what John Perry said is second-hand. We would hesitate to conclude that our acquaintance X is over-concerned about dirt if our evidence is no more than a statement by Y: 'X said that the hotels there were dirty and expensive.' We cannot now be sure whether the setting of X's remark was more like the first sequence above or the second, or indeed whether it is Y and not X who attaches importance to dirt and expense; Y may suffer himself from a morbid preoccupation by thoughts about dirt. Alternatively Y may wish to support a contention that X is a philistine. Similarly, those who have reported John Perry's statements may themselves have experienced conflicts in their relationships with mother or brother, or they may have wished, for other reasons, to support a contention that he was a rogue.

Reported statements may be misleading. The reporting by one person about another tends to be selective in such a way as to support the former's conception of the latter. A contemporary Conservative, who regards all Socialists as irresponsible in economic affairs, for instance, tends to select those statements by his opponents which appear to display such irresponsibility. In this way he preserves for himself, and perhaps for his hearers, what may well be a false conception of Socialists. Again, there is many an earnest don who has an undeserved reputation for flippancy because his friends for some reason prefer to recount those incidents in which he has appeared to lack gravity. We can have no confidence that John Perry's statements have not been misrepresented in order to preserve a conception of him which meets the needs of those who have reported them. Whatever the facts may be, he has repeatedly been cast for a part which those who have written about him have wanted him to play.

This last point is not an idle one, for we can be sure that many of those who have written about the Perrys were highly prejudiced. There seems to have been a general need to believe in their wickedness. The pamphleteer, for in, stance, made use of their story as an occasion for a homily on the prevalence and wickedness of witches and the goodness of God. He seems not to have noticed that there were gross inconsistencies in the confessions and accusations of John Perry and, after Harrison's return, that they had been exe, cuted for a crime they did not commit. He entertained no doubts about their guilt, his prejudice, the reasons for which are obscure, being sustained even when events made their innocence certain. His prejudice was widely shared, and it is indeed remarkable, as Lord Maugham has pointed out (p. 34), that there was no outcry or judicial inquiry after Harrison's return, and that extant references to a startling mis, carriage of justice were so few and late.

Sir Christopher Turnor, the judge at the Assizes of September 1660, seems to have been fair-minded, for he re, fused to convict the Perrys of murder, because there was no proof of the death of the alleged victim. Probably he carried public opinion with him. At the Assizes in the following March, however, Sir Robert Hyde accepted the jury's verdict that they were guilty and sentenced them to death. That he did so argues that he was so greatly prejudiced against the Perrys that he paid heed neither to the lack of proof, nor to the absurdities in John Perry's accusations. Possibly, public opinion had hardened against them in the interval between the Assizes. Once he had sentenced them, and they had been executed, he had a stronger and more obvious reason to wish to preserve the view that they were guilty. Presumably this was his motive when he committed to prison the man who brought to Gloucester the news of William Harrison's return.

We can hardly suppose that the failure on the part of many others to recognize the innocence of the Perrys was due to reluctance to admit that a grave mistake had been made. There must have been strong prejudices against them. Other' wise the mistake would not have been made, for it is not a sufficient explanation to suppose that Sir Robert Hyde was a bad judge. There must have been factors in the early 1660's which made people so quick to condemn Joan Perry as a witch, and John Perry as a rogue, and yet so slow to enter' tain suspicions of William Harrison. The Perrys were of the servant class. No doubt it was not less usual in Restoration times than it is today for those of position to feel threatened by the depravity and greed of servants, and to be ready to attribute wickedness to servants when they would not do so to their peers. Probably, however, there were other circum' stances which caused the Perrys to be so uncritically con' demned; they are to be found perhaps in their social and political position.

Whatever these circumstances may have been, the frag' mentary accounts of the events at Chipping Campden which now remain to us must be regarded as selective and biased.

They might be examined to discover, therefore, not so much what kind of person John Perry was as what kind of person he was conceived to be. Yet the bare bones of the story are reasonably reliable. John Perry brought about the death by hanging of his mother, his brother, and himself because he accused them and himself of the murder of William Harrison. Having disappeared in the night of 16 August, William Harrison reappeared two years later and told a strange, incredible tale to explain his absence. His reappearance makes it certain that John Perry's accusations were false.

These events held a peculiar interest at the time at which they took place. Three centuries later they can still arouse the interest of countless readers. The persistent curiosity about them is much more than that likely to be aroused by an example of the miscarriage of justice. We must suppose, therefore, that they contain elements which exert a special fascination. For many of those who have felt this fascination, the essence of the mystery lies in the false accusations made by a son against his mother and brother, and apparently calculated to bring about their death and his own death. For others it lies in the disappearance of an elderly steward for two years in times of political upheaval.

II

John Perry was responsible for the death of his mother, as well as for that of his brother, although perhaps responsible in a lesser degree than if he had stabbed or poisoned her. At any rate, he seems to have willed her death and to have regarded her as deserving to die by hanging. He took no step to save her. To this extent he was guilty of matricide.

As criminal statistics show, matricide is a relatively rare

event; so is fratricide. Opportunities for psychological study of murderers of this kind are even rarer, since such cases as do occur are dealt with by courts of justice, who tend to ask no more of the psychiatrist than an opinion on the defendant's sanity. No systematic study of matricide is to be found in the psychiatric literature, but there are a small number of case reports.[1] Yet matricide is of great interest to psychiatrists, not least because of its bearing on Freud's theory of the Oedipus complex. However, several of those who have discussed it have depended, not on actual cases, but on such literary cases as Aeschylus' or Euripides' story of Orestes or Shakespeare's story of Hamlet, which have perhaps the advantage that the murderer's motives are subjected to a more profound analysis than has usually been achieved in actual cases. Another notable case is that of Nero. If the reader will allow that Hamlet was also responsible for his mother's death, the Hamlet story is of special relevance to our consideration of John Perry's motives, and has been illuminated by many critics, notably from a psychological point of view by Ernest Jones.[2]

By bringing together such facts as can be found in the literature, although they are few, we can hazard the following description of one type of matricide. The patient has more often been a son than a daughter; the murder of a mother by her daughter has also been reported, but is still less common. He has usually been in his teens or early twenties, that is, over the age of puberty, but still young. He has been unmarried, and usually has shown little or no interest in women as sexual partners. He has appeared to be

[1] e.g. F. Wertham, *Dark Legend* (1947).
[2] *Hamlet and Oedipus* (1949).

closely attached to his mother, and she to him, although to a lesser degree. His father has been absent from the home because of death, desertion, or divorce, but his father's place by his mother's side has usually been taken in some degree of intimacy by another man. Wertham's patient, who was seventeen years old when he stabbed his mother to death, was the oldest child, and his father died when the patient was eleven years old, that is, shortly before his puberty. It is probable that this case is typical in both these respects.

There is usually no history of delinquency. On the contrary, the patient has been most scrupulous and has held to high moral standards. He has shown no symptoms of mental illness until shortly before he has committed the murder—Orestes and Hamlet were exceptional in this respect. Even then the symptoms have not been florid. He has known, in the words of the McNaghten rules, 'the nature and quality of the act he was doing', and that it was 'contrary to law', although he has regarded it as justified by his mother's unfaithfulness to his father. His belief in her guilt in this respect has been delusional, although it may also have had a substantial basis in reality. Usually he has felt that he has had some complicity in the sins for which he judges her. Usually he has premeditated the murder, and may have planned it for a relatively long time, although he has shown vacillation and uncertainty in his feelings towards her. After her death he has shown, in several cases, no regret and has been strikingly little disturbed by his crime and its consequences; in some cases he has shown profound remorse and self-reproach. In some cases he has murdered, or attempted to murder, the man who in his belief has taken his father's place.

The explanations given in the psychiatric literature in most cases centre largely on Freud's theory of the Oedipus complex. The explanation of John Perry's matricide, now to be gradually elaborated, follows the same lines, although it places the emphasis somewhat differently and attaches less specific importance to this aspect of the relationships of a child with his parents than would an orthodox psycho-analytic explanation. Leaving brothers and sisters out of consideration, the relationships in a family, when these are harmonious, may be thought of as forming a triangle, the base of which is a close, mutually satisfying bond between the mother and father. The child, who forms the apex of the triangle, is born into a closely knit group of two. The father now shares the mother's affections with their son, and accepts the diversion of her affections from himself in so far as he regards the child as an extension of himself. That is, potential rivalry with the child is resolved through 'identification'. The father's greater powers and his precedence oblige the son to accept the father's special position in the mother's affections. At puberty the triangle of relationships undergoes change. There is then a revival of the son's sexual feelings which enter again into his relationship with his mother. In some degree these are reduced through the strengthening of his identification with his father, and in some degree they are diverted into a relationship, which the mother allows or encourages, with another woman, who is at first a substitute for the mother. In psychoanalytic theory the essence of the child's relationship with his mother, both before and after puberty, is sexual. Strong prohibitions against incestuous desires, however, transform the relationship through the mechanisms of repression.

Conflicts arise when the base of the triangle is defective, especially when this is due to the sudden loss of the father by death or desertion. They are likely to be more severe still if the relationship between the mother and father fails for this or for some other reason at about the time of the son's puberty. The normal reorganization in his relationships with his parents and others at this time then becomes seriously distorted. In Wertham's case, for instance, the son had begun to identify fairly strongly with his father, and when his father died he took over his father's place in fantasy. Having done so, he felt rejected by his mother when she took lovers, of whom he became intensely jealous. His frustrated feelings then became transformed into a strong condemnation of his mother for her unfaithfulness to his father. The conflicts to which he was subjected became unendurable, and the matricide may be regarded as his attempt to resolve them.

Similarly, 'the main theme' of the Hamlet story, Ernest Jones has said,[1] 'is a highly elaborated and disguised account of a boy's love for his mother and consequent jealousy of and hatred towards his father', this hatred being displaced on to his uncle. The normal reorganization of his relationships at puberty was disturbed, we must suppose, and the close relationship with his mother persisted. Harbouring strong incestuous desires for her, hitherto repressed, he became profoundly disturbed by her incest with his uncle, and her complicity in the murder of his father. His knowledge of his mother's and uncle's part in the death of his father, and their adultery, came from the Ghost, it should be noted. It would be difficult to decide to what class of phenomena the Ghost should be assigned, but it would be possible to maintain that

[1] p. 143.

it was an hallucination and, therefore, that his knowledge was delusional, being derived, not from experiences of the real world, but from fantasy experiences accepted as veridical. The story ends with the death of his mother, his uncle, and himself; in this way he avenged the murder of his father, with whom he had identified. This is a different story from that of Oedipus. Indeed, there are many cases of matricide which do not conform to the Oedipus legend. A sixteen-year-old girl, for instance, carried out a premeditated attack on her mother and killed her. The parents had separated by agreement a year or so earlier. Although she lived with her mother, she took the father's side, regarding him as deeply injured, and condemned her mother.

Unfortunately we know nothing of John Perry's father, and in particular nothing of the quality of his father's relationship with his mother, except that at the relevant time she had been a widow for three years.[1] John was the younger of two children, being born seven years after Richard and being 25 years old at his death. We are told that John 'even from a youth did dwell with Mr. Harrison', but we do not know why he moved from his parents' house or the circumstances in which he did so. It seems reasonable to suppose, however, that this was a crucial experience for him, whether it occurred near his puberty or at some other time, and that it aroused feelings that he was rejected by his mother. Such feelings would not easily be relieved, and would exert a powerful influence upon his attitudes towards the members

[1] The entries from the parish registers which may be supposed to refer to these Perrys are given, with others, in P. C. Rushen, *History of Campden* (n.d. ? 1911), p. 66. Richard, son of Richard Perry, baptized 15 Mar. 1628/9; John, son of Richard Perry, baptized 7 Feb. 1635/6; Richard Perry (presumably the father), buried 9 Oct. 1657.

of his family. It is likely that nevertheless he continued to feel strongly attached to his mother. It is probably of significance that he did not marry, whereas Richard married and had two children. In these circumstances his father's death would have been a disturbing event, for it would have re-aroused the conflicts in his relationships with his mother and brother. He might then have felt impelled to seek from her the affection which previously he had felt himself denied. Yet it seems that it was Richard, the older son, who was preferred, and who took his father's place at his mother's side; John was again dismissed. In these conjectures we have an explanation why John should harbour strong feelings of resentment against his mother and brother.

We must suppose that he felt strong resentment; otherwise he would not have brought about their deaths. Masefield depicts John as the unsuccessful rival of his brother who, although the younger, had been earning eight shillings a week against John's seven, and who found greater favour with his mother, Mr. Harrison, and others. John, on the other hand, was a 'drunken dog', who felt himself at a disadvantage. 'You was born to tread on my corns, you was, you closhy put', he says to Richard in Masefield's play (p. 79), and of him (p. 80), 'But I will mind him, I tell 'ee; He have crossed me since we weren't that high.' Rivals in many things, they were also rivals for the position held by their father in their mother's affections and then vacated. More desirous, but ousted, John suffered the frustration of strong feelings towards his mother. Whether these feelings were essentially sexual is a point for psychologists to argue amongst themselves, and is immaterial here.

We may further conjecture that William Harrison became

something of a father to John, as well as being his 'Master', and 'did love him well'. Let us also suppose that John Perry was not a party to his disappearance, and that, with others, he believed him to be dead. Might he not then believe, as Hamlet did, that the usurper of his real father's place, his successful rival, and his unfaithful mother had murdered him, and that he too was implicated in their crime? Such beliefs were not rational, but they might have arisen, just as Hamlet's did, out of the disturbance produced by an un-resolved Oedipus complex, or, more generally, out of the unresolved conflicts in his relationship with his mother.

This explanation of the mystery of John Perry's accusa-tions and confession is highly speculative, and we can now hardly expect that new evidence will emerge which will corroborate it, but it is compatible with the scanty facts known to us; nothing known to us is in conflict with it. It assumes that John regarded William Harrison as a father in such a degree that his putative death aroused fantasies like those, expressed so freely by Hamlet, which have their origins in a son's guilt-ridden desire to dispose of his father and to enjoy an exclusive relationship with his mother. This assumption is not an unreasonable one. Fantasies like those associated with the Oedipus complex are not uncommonly aroused by bereavements when the patient's relationship with his mother has been as conflictful as we suppose John Perry's to have been.

John Perry's accusations against his mother and brother were derived from fantasies and not from memories of real experiences, although he reported them as derived from real experiences. The reader might ask whether he realized that their origins were in fantasies, and that they were not veridical. Had he done so, they might properly be described as lies. Similar accusations against parents are occasionally made, it is true, by so-called 'pathological liars', although the crimes mentioned are then more often sexual than aggressive, but even these patients rarely have more than a dim appreciation that their accusations are derived from fantasies. In so far as their origin in fantasies is not recognized, and they are regarded as veridical, they are delusional. Anyhow, the distinction between lies and delusions has little psychological significance. John Perry's accusations, we suppose, arose out of conflicts which are subjected to severe repression, and are the source of intense anxiety. It is highly unlikely, therefore, that he would have had more than a vague awareness of their origins. He might have doubted whether they were rational, just as Hamlet entertained doubts about his uncle's and mother's crimes, but he would have felt that they were true. He acted accordingly.

John Perry believed William Harrison to be dead, we suppose, and he had had no warning. The manner and the rate with which his delusions evolved during the first few weeks is fully compatible with the explanation that has been proposed. At first he put forward rational explanations, that William Harrison had been killed by a tinker or by a gentleman's servant living in the neighbourhood. Only after a week under severe stress did he disclose, before the justice of the peace on Friday, 24 August, his belief in the guilt of his mother and brother. This gradual development of delusions over several days is typical. They tend to change rapidly when they first emerge, and to become fixed and stereotyped only gradually if they persist. Self-reproach tends to be predominant at the beginning, and then to fade slowly, while accusations against others become more definite for a time. The patient may then come to believe that he too is a victim of their attacks. Typical in this respect is John Perry's assertion at the September Assizes that 'his mother and brother had attempted to poison him in the jail, so that he durst neither eat or drink with them'.

As time passes the patient may express paranoid delusions of this kind less freely, and become more aware of the irrationality of much that he has said. Nevertheless, although his delusions are less expressed, and he achieves a degree of insight, his hostile attitudes towards those whom he has accused may harden. These changes seem to have taken place in the case of John Perry in the interval between the Assizes. At the September Assizes he repeated the account of the murder, which he had given to the justice of the peace on 24 August, but at the March Assizes he expressed no delusions and realized that he had been mad. He told them, 'He was then mad, and knew not what he said.' Yet he continued to condemn, albeit tacitly, his mother and brother until immediately before his own death.

The course in the case of Hamlet was similar. His 'turbulent and dangerous lunacy' in Act III abated and in Act V, scene 2 he spoke to Laertes of his 'sore distraction' and said 'What I have done . . . I here proclaim was madness.' Yet within a short time, through the inevitable march of events, he witnessed his mother's death and killed his uncle, the 'murderous, damned Dane', as he called him.

Just before he died, John Perry retracted his accusations. For this retraction our explanation does not account, nor does it account for his prediction that 'they might hereafter (possibly) hear'. However, its failure at this point, although a weakness, does not make it untenable. He might well have entertained a rational explanation of William Harri-son's disappearance, although he retained a firm delusional conviction that his mother and brother were guilty of murder. Deluded patients not uncommonly express in-compatible ideas one after the other.

John Perry's emotional responses at various times between the day of Harrison's disappearance and the execution several months later would almost certainly have revealed his abnormality. It is unlikely that they would have been ob-served accurately, and Sir Thomas Overbury tells us noth-ing of his demeanour during the crucial week following Harrison's disappearance. It would be expected that he would have shown intense anxiety during the first few days while his delusions were evolving, and that then his anxiety would have subsided, to be replaced by a dull per-plexity without apparent distress. This state might well have been judged at the time to be one of indifference, strikingly inappropriate to the gravity of his situation and to his accusations, which would have been taken at their face value, without appreciation of their value in resolving his Oedipal conflicts. He would have continued in a dull, withdrawn, apathetic state until his death. The description of him at the place of execution as having 'a dogged and surly carriage' fits well.

That much of what John Perry said to the justice of the peace was absurd and contradictory is not evidence against the view that it was delusional. On the contrary, delu-sions are often absurd and contradictory. In some respects, however, his confession was not typically delusional. Thus, as reported by Sir Thomas Overbury, it appears to have been too coherent and too complete, and to have contained too many circumstantial details. Delusions tend to be like caricatures, rather than drawings, for they tend to lack ordinary details. The few details they contain tend to be incongruous and to have an extravagant emphasis. However, we do not know for certain in what terms he expressed himself, for the only account available to us was written probably much later by Sir Thomas Overbury. It is likely that any incoherence would have been reduced in the reporting. Furthermore, a substantial part of the confession was probably derived from real experience, such as his meeting with John Pierce and his visit to the hen-roost. On the other hand, the murder in the Conygree was certainly delusional. Whether he had really plotted with his brother to rob Mr. Harrison, or whether he had been responsible for the planting of the hat, comb, and band, is quite uncertain.

John Perry's story, told 'not many weeks before Harrison's absence' . . . 'how he had been set upon by two men in white with naked swords, and how he had defended himself with his sheep pick', is more typically delusional, for it contains extravagant and incongruous details—the men in white, the naked swords, and the cuts on the handle of the pick and on the key in his pocket, for instance. Its quality is that of a dream experience. Indeed, we may suppose that he had just awoken from a nightmare and, recalling dream experiences, had mistaken them for real experiences. Mistakes like this are often made by normal people. Waking from a dream, imaginations are recalled which are as vivid as perceptions. Strong doubts are felt for a time whether the events recalled have really happened. Eventually they are dismissed as imaginations, although without any sense of conviction, because they are in conflict with other knowledge. Sometimes, however, the misinterpretation of imaginations as perceptions is not corrected, and becomes the basis of persistent delusions.

Had there been evidence to show that John Perry's misinterpretation of a dream experience as veridical had continued for more than a short time after he came running, 'seemingly frightened', out of Campden garden, and that 'reality testing' had failed to correct it, we might have concluded that he was deluded before William Harrison's disappearance. But the evidence is to the contrary, for at his first trial he was quite clear that he had not been attacked, although he also gave then what was almost certainly a false and misleading explanation of the incident.

This incident may, therefore, be dismissed as having little significance in arriving at a diagnosis of John Perry, although it may have made a substantial contribution to the popular conception of him as a rogue. The main components of his dream, the men in white and the naked swords, are such suggestive symbols that it is tempting to argue that they indicate the reawakening of his conflicts in his relationships with his mother and brother, but this or any other interpretation of the dream would be rash on the slender evidence available to us.

There now remain a number of questions which have to do with the diagnostic label to be attached to John Perry. Was he a rogue? If one wished to argue that he was, one would point to his part as an accessory to his brother in breaking into William Harrison's house and stealing £140 in money. To these offences he pleaded guilty at his first trial, when he was pardoned under the Act of Oblivion, but he denied his guilt afterwards. In his confession to the examining magistrate and at his first trial he admitted planning to rob William Harrison at other times. Moreover, he said many things which were untrue. Even taken altogether, these are still slight grounds for regarding him as a rogue, and, for the reasons already given, we need not accept the judgements made on him by his contemporaries. Sir John Collie[1] inclined towards the diagnosis of 'moral insanity', which amounts to a similar charge, but the reasons he gave for doing so are unimpressive. In any event, the term 'moral insanity' is an outmoded and unsatisfactory one. Its contemporary counterpart is 'psychopathic personality', but the most weighty evidence in favour of this description of him is his callous indifference to the fate of his mother and brother, and for this we have proposed a different, more reasonable explanation.

Was he mad? One might as well ask: Was Hamlet mad? The latter question has been the subject of much fruitless discussion (but *vide* Jones, 1949). Neither question is a satisfactory one, for 'mad', 'insane', or 'of unsound mind' have no precise meaning, except when the criteria are given by the context, as they are, for instance, when the question of admission under certificate to a mental hospital arises, or previously when the defending Counsel entered a plea of insanity in a murder charge. Thus a more appropriate, although hypothetical, question is: Would John Perry have been certifiable as a person of unsound mind under the

[1] 'The Case of John Perry' in *Transactions of the Medico-Legal Society*, xx (1926), 105–20.

provisions of the Lunacy Act of 1890? To this question we can confidently answer: No.

He did not murder William Harrison, although he was found guilty of doing so and executed. He was responsible for the death of his mother and brother, although he was not guilty of their murder in a legal sense. It would be foolish to ask, therefore, whether a plea of insanity in accordance with the McNaghten Rules would have been acceptable. Were we to put this question, however, the answer would again be No, for, although he was suffering from an 'insane delusion respecting one or more particular persons' and he was acting in revenge of some supposed injury, he knew what he was doing and that it was wrong.

We suppose that he was profoundly disturbed by conflicts arising out of his relationship with his mother, and that he was deluded. Was he also suffering from a psychosis? A definite answer cannot be given, but it seems most probable that he developed an acute psychosis during the first few days after William Harrison's disappearance, and this psychosis persisted until his death, although the more florid symptoms subsided in the interval between the Assizes. Did this illness belong to the class of psychosis to which previously the label 'dementia precox' would have been attached and which would now be called 'schizophrenia'? If we were pressed to give an answer, we would make a formal diagnosis of schizophrenia, although we would hasten to add, as is usual today, that the concept of schizophrenia is a quite unsatisfactory one, although the diagnosis still has a certain usefulness because it indicates what are the main symptoms.

These questions of the diagnostic label are unprofitable, however, and the reader is advised not to concern himself with them, but to ponder on the psychological processes which can make a young man accuse his mother and brother of a crime they have not committed and condemn them to die, and which enable him to witness their execution with surly passivity.[1] These are the processes which in some circumstances knit individuals together into a harmonious and beneficent family, but which in other circumstances bring them to destroy each other. The transformation of constructive into destructive forces, which has recurred over and over again throughout the centuries as a dramatic theme, is a main component of John Perry's story, and the component to which it largely owes its fascination.

III

Writing in 1676 Sir Thomas Overbury describes William Harrison at the time of his disappearance in 1660 as 'being about seventy years of age', 'in his old age', and 'an old and infirm man'. It is doubtful, however, whether he was then as old and infirm as Overbury suggests. He continued to sign the Chipping Campden Grammar School accounts regularly after his return until 1672, or at any rate as regularly as any of the other governors, since he signed on 12 out of 17 possible occasions. Moreover, Overbury wrote of him in 1676 as if he was still alive. Presumably, too, he was in at least fair health in 1660, since he went out himself to demand rents at Charringworth more than three miles away. Overbury further described him as being of good reputation as 'a just and faithful servant' and 'sober in life and conversation'. As Lord Maugham remarks (p. 87),

[1] See, for instance, I. D. Suttie, *The Origins of Love and Hate* (1935).

we know nothing about his relationships with his wife and son at the time of his disappearance.

In trying to decide what kind of person William Harrison was we have one advantage which we do not have in our study of John Perry. Overbury reproduced in his tract Harrison's written statement verbatim, whereas his report of John Perry's confession is a summary of an oral examination by the justice of the peace. Presumably Harrison's letter was neither amended nor edited. One thing about this letter is reasonably certain. It was written by a man with all his faculties intact, for it provides a clear, detailed, and coherent although incomplete narrative of a lengthy series of events. It shows no signs of mental impairment at all. This conclusion stands whether its content is true or fabrication.

There are no significant differences in Harrison's signatures on the school accounts after his return. That is, there is nothing in the signatures to suggest any deterioration in him then. The first signature after his return, that on 15 October 1663, is rather bolder than its predecessors, but this difference was not sustained and was probably a casual variation. His last signature on 16 April 1672 showed some deterioration perhaps; if so, it was due most likely to senility.

The quality of his letter and his signatures after his return, and his survival for at least another ten years, allow us to dismiss any suggestion that his strange tale was a 'confabulation' which filled in a gap in his memory due to a disease of the brain. This was at most a remote possibility. Patients who have suffered from a disease of the brain whether due to alcoholic intoxication, infection, a stroke, or other cause, occasionally give, after the acute phase of their illness has passed, a rich and detailed account of fictitious events, but, when they do so in written form, they display easily recognized signs of mental impairment, such as faulty syntax, faulty spelling, faulty use of words, and incompatible details set side by side, as well as incoherence and lack of orderliness in the description of sequences of events. None of these signs is apparent in Harrison's letter. In any event, there seems to have been no indication whatever that he was ill in this way at the time of his disappearance.

If a man of seventy years of age leaves his occupation, home, and family for two years, mental illness, such as a depression, is one possible reason. Had he been mentally ill during his absence, Harrison, as a man of some substance, would have been looked after privately in a house in the neighbourhood, or, for that matter, in another part of the country, but it is very unlikely that his whereabouts would have remained undisclosed, and it is also very unlikely that he would have told such a strange tale on his return.

Harrison's letter shows some curious features, which deserve mention, although their significance is uncertain. Perhaps its most remarkable feature is that it tells us so little about him as a person. It gives hardly a hint of distress, discouragement, or despair in terrible misfortunes and hardships, or of anger at those responsible for them or hope of deliverance or gratitude for help. It makes no accusations and passes no judgements. The writer might have been a passive and unfeeling spectator, for all the emotion it displays.

Especially, its description of the attack on him and the journey across England contain strikingly few of the explanations that are usual in narrative. Note that the first few events recorded are given explanations. He went to Charringworth, he wrote, 'to demand rents'. He stayed there 'till the close of the evening, because the tenants were busy in the fields and late when they came home'. He *expected* a considerable sum. But after the clause, 'fearing he would ride over me', there are very few reasons given for events which cry out for explanation. This lack is less evident in the description of the journey home. They undertook to transport him, he wrote, 'for my bowl'. Of the men who came out of a ship of Hamburg he wrote, 'they durst not, for fear of being discovered by the Searchers', and of one of the Gentlemen in Lisbon, 'taking compassion on me'.

We may conclude accordingly that the description of the journey across England refers to events which were not normally experienced. We cannot conclude, however, that it was a fabrication, although it may have been, for it is possible that the events occurred but that Harrison did not experience them normally because he was ill as a result of his injuries and exhaustion. The rest of the letter explains so little that needs explaining and leaves out so much, that it is hardly acceptable as a frank and true account. But there is nothing in it that helps us towards a diagnosis of William Harrison.

INDEX

PRINTED IN GREAT BRITAIN
AT THE UNIVERSITY PRESS, OXFORD
BY VIVIAN RIDLER
PRINTER TO THE UNIVERSITY